Not "Just a Salad"

NOT "JUST A SALAD"

How to Eat Well and Stay Healthy When Dining Out

Cheryl Sindell

FOREWORD BY
Wolfgang Puck

PHAROS BOOKS
A SCRIPPS HOWARD COMPANY
NEW YORK

Publisher's Note: Although *Not "Just a Salad"* tells which foods to choose and provides tips, up-to-the-minute knowledge, and clear answers about restaurant eating, weight loss, and nutrition, it does not replace professional advice. To understand your nutritional circumstances and determine to what degree you should adhere to each dietary health principle, consult with a registered dietitian or a physician knowledgeable about nutrition.

The author wishes to thank the following restaurants for their kind permission to reprint their menus in *Not "Just a Salad"*: La Tour Restaurant, An American Place, La Scala Presto Trattoria, Naturally Fast, The Plum Tree Inn, Noma Restaurant, Taste of India, Papadakis Taverna.

Library of Congress Cataloging-in-Publication Data

Sindell, Cheryl.
Not "just a salad" : how to eat well and stay healthy when eating out / by Cheryl Sindell.
p. cm.
Includes index.
ISBN 0-88687-733-4 : $10.95
1. Low-calorie diet. 2. Restaurants. 3. Low-cholesterol diet. 4. Diet therapy. I. Title.
RM222.2.S557 1993
613.2—dc20 92-37952
CIP

Designed by Claire Counihan

Pharos Books
A Scripps Howard Company
200 Park Avenue
New York, NY 10166

10 9 8 7 6 5 4 3 2 1
First Edition

This book is dedicated to four of the special people I am privileged to have in my life. Leslie Kallen and I conceived the *Not "Just a Salad"* concept in a restaurant one evening while deciding what to order for dinner. Her friendship and encouragement made my work easier while writing this book and my life sweeter.

Gerry Schick, MSW, helped me believe in my dream to write in spite of how difficult it is to get a first book published. Our relationship gave me the courage to get this project off the ground and follow through.

My love forever to Robert Heller, M.D., my husband. He shared his knowledge of food as it relates to good health, and gave this book the strong foundation it is built upon. He also gave his love, support, and friendship. He'd take me out to dinner when I didn't have time to cook, wanted to relax, or needed to do more research.

This book is also dedicated to Chelsea, my daughter, who sits at the computer with me and continuously brightens my life with her ideas, enthusiasm, and smile.

Man can live without poetry,
  music, and art,
Man can live without conscience,
  live without heart . . .
Women can live without love,
  what is passion but pining?
But show me the man or woman,
  that can live without dining.

—*Owen Meredith*

Contents

▲

Acknowledgments

▲

MY gratitude to the thousands of clients I've counseled who were sick and tired of deprivation diets and ready to enjoy themselves while eating out and staying healthy. With all my heart, I thank Paula Derrington, Ph.D.; Michele Montano, Joan Follendore and Sandy Rose for reading and critiquing my work before anyone else saw it. Their comments and encouragement kept me going throughout the duration of this project.

Many people at Pharos Books and Knightsbridge Publishing Company breathed life into this book. I particularly want to thank Hana Lane and Shelly Usen, my editors, for seeing the potential for *Not "Just a Salad"* and making it more readable. And thanks to Lisa Wyeth Kirk, Kathy Freedland, Mina Freehill, Fred Goss, Ellen Komp, and other essential players on the team who contributed their expertise and good taste. A special nod to my copy editor, Sona Vogel, and to my proofreader, Sheryl Strauss, for doing an extraordinary job.

I also want to thank the many people who helped me with the foreign languages used in *Not "Just a Salad"*. They include: M. Monique Simms, Severine Hafah, Christina Rodriguis, T. Shook Ko, C.A.; Jo-Lien Wong, Yasue Harada, Nadia Baker, Giovanni Aponte, Ph.D.; Jai Joseph, Johnny Papadakis, Katherine Neumann, M.D.; Bobby Sookoo, and Rita Kumar, M.D.

My appreciation to the many restaurateurs who permitted me to reprint their menus, and to the Metropolitan Life Insurance Company for allowing me to use their desirable weights chart.

Special thanks go out to Elmer Dills, Nina Hull, Bushra Rothstein, Ph.D.; Wolfgang Puck, Linda Seger, Ph.D.; Justin Brisk, Fernando Montes, Kellee Blanchard and Leonard Ota at Nikko Inflight Catering Services for the information they provided.

And finally, I want to thank Leonard Ledler, Ph.D. I wish every writer could have a friend as supportive as Lenny. He was my first writing teacher and has been a mentor to me throughout the process of writing this book.

Foreword

▲

WHEN I was in my twenties, I didn't associate pleasing my customers with good business. If someone wanted a dish prepared a special way—a veal chop without the sauce, for example—I told the waiters to say, "No, the chef's not going to do it." But I got insults. People wanted to know why they could get the dish prepared the way they wanted it at another good restaurant, but not at mine. I would get upset, the waiter would get upset, and the customer would get upset. Then I realized my mistake. It would cost me less money if I didn't have to make the sauce, it would make the customer happy, and he would come back the next week. Now I stress flexibility in all of my restaurants.

Today, there's every reason people can eat a healthy meal in almost any restaurant. And, obviously, the better the restaurant, the more accommodating the chef will be. Nowadays, a customer can make a special request and if the chef says, "No, that's not how I make it," the customer will just leave.

Many customers, however, are embarrassed or scared to ask for something different. They should realize that the menu is not the Ten Commandments! *Not "Just a Salad"* encourages people to make special requests and helps them get into the habit of ordering healthful foods.

As our tendency toward healthy dining continues, I see many trends that are reflected in this book. Ethnic foods are becoming more popular. They are more health-oriented and are much less expensive, because they contain more vegetables, less meat, and many more herbs, spices, and vinegars. Consumers are becoming more aware of ingredients, buying leaner cuts of meat, and looking for organic fruits and vegetables. Fifteen years ago, what kinds of salad ingredients or vegetables could you get in the supermarkets? Not a large variety. Now, you can find almost anything you want in most supermarkets and at farmers' markets.

People are learning about balance. Instead of just jumping on the bandwagon to buy one particular product—like oat bran—they are realizing that there's no one magical food. And people see that they can be on a healthy eating plan and still eat the foods they like in moderation.

Many of my customers are learning how to order meals that will be good for them. They know they can't eat steak, lobster, or fish with sauce every day, so they're careful. They might order angel hair pasta with skinless chicken breast in a tomato base, followed by risotto with wild mushrooms and vegetables, without butter or cheese, and fresh-fruit sorbet for dessert.

We know now what dishes contain a lot of fat—beef, lamb, butter, cheese. We know what foods contribute to high cholesterol. And we know we can go to a restaurant, eat the foods that are good for us, and still walk away feeling satisfied.

Not "Just a Salad" points the way to *successful* dining. Use it, enjoy it, and *bon appétit!*

—***Wolfgang Puck***

Preface

▲

I REMEMBER thinking in 1974, it wasn't long ago that heads turned when I walked into a room. Now they turn away when I'm wheeled into the corridor.

In 1974, I came down with Guillain-Barré Syndrome (GBS), a disease that attacks the nervous system and causes paralysis. It's the same illness that Joseph Heller and Speed Vogel wrote about in *No Laughing Matter*. Believe me, that's an appropriate title. You can die from Guillain-Barré, recover completely, or be left with residual paralysis.

After the disease overtook me I could no longer work, because I couldn't walk, write, or even turn the pages of a book. The illness caused complete paralysis of my arms and legs. After two hospitalizations I moved to my parents' home so they could take care of me. Fortunately, my insurance paid eighty percent of the medical bills.

In an attempt to reverse this disease, my doctor, Louis Rosner, prescribed high doses of a medication called prednisone, a cortisone-based drug; it caused an acnelike rash and "moon-face"—extreme bloating of my face. Although I was eating moderate amounts of a variety of fresh foods—and very little fat, salt, or sugar—over a three-month period I gained forty-five pounds. I could barely recognize myself in the mirror, and both strangers and friends turned away.

Before GBS, I'd had a preoccupation with slimness. Every day after teaching school, I went to the neighborhood gym to exercise and sweat with other women. After class we talked about dieting while measuring our thighs. At our local health bar, we ate low-calorie "Weight Watchers" malts, Jell-O made from artificially sweetened soda, and chocolate cookies made with Sweet'n Low, chocolate flavoring, and shredded apples. These low-calorie snacks were the only foods we felt comfortable eating away from home.

The reality of being paralyzed and sentenced to a wheelchair, possibly for the rest of my life, gave me a lot of time to think about why being thin had been so important to me. Dieting, after all, caused me emotional suffering, lowered my resistance to disease, and interfered with one of life's greatest pleasures—eating out.

That realization was the beginning of a year-long recovery period. With the use of a mechanical page turner, I read extensively about the relationship between food and health. In my studies I found tremendous amounts of misinformation and contradiction about what's best to eat. Through further extensive research I separated the good advice about nutrition from the bad and sometimes even dangerous.

I put myself on a healthy, lifelong eating plan. And with the help of a few strong friends, I was able to get to restaurants. Eating out was extremely important to me, because it was one of the few ways I could socialize. In restaurants I learned that if I ordered carefully, I could stay on my plan and eat only delicious, nutritious, low-fat, high-fiber foods, prepared in a healthful manner without a lot of sugar or salt.

One day, both to my doctor's astonishment and to my own amazement, I had a hint of recovery. Upon command, I moved one toe just barely. I could hardly believe it wasn't a muscle twitch, but I knew it was my brain signaling my body to move and my body responding to the message. I had made it happen! However, the next time I tried to move that toe, it wouldn't move. For three days, I kept signaling with no response. Then that tiny toe moved again.

I continued on my sound nutritional plan to build my

strength, and after seeing a physical therapist four times a week for six months, I could finally "shuffle walk." I was able to leave my parents' home and take care of my own necessities. By "eating smart" and doing the moderate exercises prescribed by the physical therapist, little by little I rebuilt my body. Over another six months, I got stronger and lost the forty-five pounds I had gained. In 1977, three years after the battle began, my doctor considered me one hundred percent recovered from Guillain-Barré Syndrome. I am lucky to be alive.

Although there is still no proven treatment or known cause for GBS, there is no doubt in my mind that the cure was a combination of prednisone, physical therapy, and eating the way I did.

After my recovery I realized my interest in slimness had turned into a preoccupation with good health, so I attended UCLA for graduate studies in health and nutrition. I wanted to simplify what I had learned and share that knowledge with others, using every form of communication.

On television I became the ABC *Eyewitness News* nutritional newscaster and a regular guest on *A. M. Los Angeles*. On KABC TALKRADIO I talked with Elmer Dills about dining out. I lectured to organizations, wrote columns in magazines and articles in newspapers, and counseled clients on a one-to-one basis. In private practice I began designing nutritional life-style plans to fit my clients' needs.

While some of the people I counsel are healthy and merely want a palatable eating plan to prevent illness, others need to lose or gain weight, lower their blood cholesterol levels, regulate diabetes or alleviate other conditions related to nutrition. No matter what their nutritional problems, all my clients wanted to know how to apply healthful eating strategies while dining in their favorite restaurants. I began to scrutinize French, Italian, Mexican, Chinese, Japanese, American, Indian, Greek, and all the other most popular cuisines, observing similarities and differences in the ingredients and cooking techniques.

After counseling thousands of clients, I decided to write this guide, *Not "Just a Salad"*, to assist people in attaining and maintaining their best weight and optimal health while eating out. Take it along. It is your guide. Keep it in your purse or briefcase if you eat out often, because it will help you protect yourself from greasy, salty, sugary, high-calorie restaurant foods.

When you learn to take charge of the preparation of your food in restaurants, you will be able to maintain sociability, eat right, and avoid the "diet suffering" I experienced for so long. Make eating out a time when family and friends meet to nourish themselves, talk, and share the events and feelings of the day.

Although I would not wish illness on anyone, had it not been for Guillain-Barré I doubt that I would have become a nutrition consultant, worked in the media, or have written *Not "Just a Salad"*.

Through personal experience, I've learned that nothing pays greater dividends than an investment in your health: looking your best, feeling energetic, and enjoying total well-being. Health is everything!

Author's Introduction

▲

A WHILE ago I was sitting in a restaurant where I could hear three conversations simultaneously. The lady at table number one said to the waiter, "I'll have the chef's salad dieter's special; I have to lose some weight." At table number two a woman said to her friend, "My doctor says I've got to say good-bye to butter and stick to a low-fat diet because there's cancer in my family history, but I don't know if it's okay to eat margarine." At table number three a man was talking with his lady friend. Apparently the gentleman had undergone a coronary bypass operation recently, and he said (while drinking coffee and eating cereal with nondairy creamer), "At least I'm not eating foods containing cholesterol anymore."

"But," replied the woman, "nondairy creamers are loaded with saturated fats, and my dietitian says they clog the arteries like cholesterol."

"Then I'm obviously confused," he said.

Actually, all three people were confused. The lady at table number one thought (as many people do) that a dieter's special, a salad, would be a good choice for anyone trying to lose weight. But because of the ham, cheese, and the fat in the dressing, a chef's salad can have more calories than a three-course meal.

The lady at table number two didn't know that although all margarines contain saturated fat, the more solid a fat is at room temperature, the more saturated it is. So, it's better to use the tub and liquid "squeeze" type margarines.

The gentleman at table number three thought he was eliminating cholesterol, but he was misinformed—most nondairy creamers contain saturated fat, and taking in too much saturated fat is just as harmful as eating too much cholesterol. In other words, products devoid of cholesterol may contain saturated fat.

If you're confused about what to order, like the people in the restaurant, I'm not surprised. Many people are baffled about nutrition because they only hear the sensational, extreme views of experts.

While it's common for some health specialists to see an issue black and others to see it white, the majority of experts usually agree, finding the answer somewhere in the middle-of-the-road gray area. We aren't often told these moderate views, however, and simple nutrition information becomes complicated and contradictory.

Not "Just a Salad" clears up the confusion. In three parts it makes nutrition information easy to understand, so you can lose weight and stay healthy while dining in your favorite restaurants:

- Part 1, "The Dining Out Dilemma," presents the problems we face eating out and provides solutions. It tells how to lose weight and order with confidence while following a 12-Step Dining Out Program.
- Part 2, "Dining Out in Your Favorite Restaurants," makes it possible to order healthful foods in French, American, Italian, Mexican, Chinese, Japanese, Indian, and Greek restaurants here and abroad and still walk away feeling satisfied. These ethnic food chapters contain Menu Commands that list low-calorie healthful foods to choose and fatty, salty, or otherwise unhealthful dishes to avoid. Menu Command even recommends healthful desserts indigenous to each cuisine.
- Part 3, "Eating Healthfully in Our Friendly Skies," suggests ordering special meals and anti–jet lag

strategies before, during, and after flying. That way you'll feel well while traveling and have the energy you need once you reach your destination.

▲

Not "Just a Salad" does not recommend that Americans trade their coffee break for a siesta or abandon happy hour for afternoon tea. It would not work well to impose the customs of any homogeneous group on our heterogeneous society.

I am suggesting, however, that we evaluate the nutritional practices of other nations and emulate their more healthful aspects. Life is one giant menu, and your choices constitute your life-style.

A person who doesn't like himself won't eat well. He either stuffs his mouth in an attempt to forget his troubles or deprives himself of food and suffers.

If you like yourself, there is no better way to show respect for your body than to sit down in a restaurant, select the most delicious, healthful foods a cuisine has to offer, and celebrate life. Never have our restaurants been as good as they are now.

We are a melting pot. Only in the United States can you find restaurants representing every nationality. Fortunately, there are healthful foods and delicious preparation methods in every cuisine, and now—with Menu Command by your side—you'll feel comfortable ordering foods from all over the world. Let's get started.

▼

PART 1

▲

The Dining Out Dilemma

▼

Chapter 1

▲

HOLD THE MAYO!

NOT long ago customers wanted to come home from restaurants stuffed to the gills after splurging on calories, and dining out was reserved for special occasions. Today, however, the measure of a good restaurant is the quality of food served rather than the quantity. Most people eat out about five hundred times a year—they eat more than half of all their meals in restaurants—and they want to feel good afterward.

If you're like most people, you eat out while traveling, when attending business lunches and dinners, or simply to avoid cooking. Eating out is a form of entertainment and a way to socialize. It's not unusual to meet for a drink, get together for lunch, or talk over a cup of coffee. And, if you're like most people, you're probably on some type of diet and need to know how to stay on your eating plan while dining out.

Perhaps you've been sticking to a diet perfectly at home, cooking carefully without a drop of butter, salt, or sugar, weighing everything first. Then, inevitably, social or business engagements come along that you can't refuse, and you blow your diet.

Or perhaps eating out is a way of life for you. Some people go to restaurants for privacy and to relax. They may like a luxurious, quiet spot. Others want to communicate. They may go out to eat for business, glamour, or excitement, and for them it's important to walk into a crowded restaurant and have the maître d' take them directly to their table without waiting. In certain circles, restaurants have become status symbols. It's important for some people to say they've been to a particular restaurant, and for others it matters where they're seen. One of the newest reasons for eating out was the "power lunch," until the "power breakfast" came along. No matter what your reason for dining out, you may as well make it an occasion to stay on your diet and feel good about yourself.

Dining While Dieting

Like most people, you probably follow a special eating plan. Perhaps you avoid high-calorie foods because you want to lose weight, or the salt shaker because your doctor has said you have high blood pressure. Or maybe you shun fatty foods because there's heart disease or cancer in your family history, or sugar because you have diabetes or hypoglycemia. Do you follow a high-fiber diet to prevent constipation or eat sensibly simply because it makes you feel well? Most people are seeking better food in restaurants. Over the years people's awarenesses have changed, because they know good nutrition will keep them healthier now and in their later years.

Fortunately, no matter what type of eating plan you follow, it's possible to eat in restaurants without concern because restaurateurs are responding to their customers' needs.

According to the pharmaceutical company Merck, Sharp, and Dohme, almost three-quarters of all diners are ordering 96 percent more fish, 86 percent more chicken, and 93 percent fewer heavy sauces.

"HOLD THE MAYO!"

Remember in the movie *Five Easy Pieces*, when Jack Nicholson walked into a coffee shop and asked for wheat toast? He changed the image for those of us who go into a restaurant knowing what we want to eat and how we want it prepared. The dialogue (by screenwriter Adrien Joyce) goes like this.

"I'd like a plain omelet, no potatoes, tomatoes instead, a cup of coffee, and wheat toast."

"No substitutions."

"Whatdya mean? You don't have any tomatoes?"

"Only what's on the menu. You can have the Number Two Plain omelet, comes with cottage fries and a roll."

"I'll make it easy as I can. I'd like an omelet, plain, a chicken salad sandwich on toast, no mayonnaise, no butter, no lettuce, with a cup of coffee."

"Number Two chicken salad sandwich. Hold the butter, lettuce and mayonnaise, with a cup of coffee. Anything else?"

"Yes. Now all you have to do is hold the chicken, bring me the toast, bring me a check for the chicken salad, and you haven't broken any rules."

"You want me to hold the chicken, huh?"

"I want you to hold it between your knees," Nicholson replied.

When eating out it may not be easy to get what you need and you may not get a happy waitress or even common courtesy, as we saw in that memorable scene. But once you know what to ask for, order with confidence, and have a determined attitude, you'll be more likely to get the foods you want.

ORDER WITH CONFIDENCE

If you feel intimidated asking for the foods and preparation methods you need to stay on your special eating plan in restaurants, follow these basic guidelines:

- Ask quickly the questions you need answered. Waiters are usually very busy, and they are usually more cooperative if you don't take up too much of their time.
- Ask for what you want in a courteous manner. You'll find that most waiters will be extremely nice and helpful.
- Ask the waiter how dishes are prepared once you have a few alternatives in mind. That way, when your meal arrives, you're not surprised by unhealthful ingredients.
- Order with confidence.
- Send food back that doesn't taste delicious or isn't prepared the way you like it. (You'll be glad when served a dish that you like.)

Restaurant Anxiety

But if you don't know what to order, you'll never be able to stay on your eating plan while dining out. Have you experienced the following scenario?

You arrive at a restaurant where you and some friends are meeting for lunch. The hostess guides your party to a table and gives out menus. You're seated less than two minutes when the waiter arrives and asks, "May I bring you a drink?"

Not willing to tolerate another salad, you say, "I'll wait until later, thanks." The others order beverages. You and your friends check the menu. You're still trying to remember what your doctor advised regarding nutrition, but you can't.

The waiter arrives with drinks and asks, "May I take your order, please?"

Sure, if I knew what I wanted, you think to yourself, still wondering if you should order a cocktail or if sparkling mineral water with lemon would do. Everyone orders—except you.

To stall for time you say, "I'd like a few more minutes to decide and a glass of water in the meantime, please."

"I'll be right back."

You have a clear-cut case of ***restaurant anxiety***. The major food groups come to mind, but they make no more sense to you now than they did when you learned about them in the sixth grade.

The waiter returns with glasses of water. You're feeling pressured, intimidated, and anxious as you notice his perturbed look. It's because he's harried, taking care of so many tables, you rationalize, but you must decide what to order.

As the waiter inquires once again about your order, you say, pointing to your friend Barry, "I'll have what he's having."

Everyone's food arrives. You and Barry are served food submarined in grease, and you wish you had ordered what Sue has. Her food looks delicious and healthy. Your meal makes you sick just looking at it, and it's obviously not nutritious. Once you obtain ordering skills, your restaurant anxiety will dissipate. But first, you need a determined attitude.

Chapter 2

▲

HAVE A DETERMINED ATTITUDE

To get the meals you want, prepared the way you like them, have a determined attitude and follow the specific strategies detailed in part 2. Soon you'll open menus with new confidence, knowing exactly what to order. Menu Command shows you the best foods to enjoy while sticking to your special eating plan and the fatty, salty, sugary foods to avoid in your favorite restaurants. But first, here are ten questions you should get in the habit of asking yourself—before the waiter comes to your table.

1. Do I want to follow my eating plan during this meal? If so, to what extent?
2. What are my special dietary needs?
3. What type of food am I in the mood to eat? (You'll feel satisfied and eat less when you eat what you want.)
4. How hungry am I?
5. What have I already eaten today?
6. What would I like to drink?

7. Did I notice a beverage or meal, while walking to my table, that I'd like to order?
8. Is there anything I feel like eating that's not on the menu? (If there's nothing on the menu you want, the chef will probably make modifications.)
9. What are my plans concerning food for the remainder of the day?
10. Does my appetite match my plans and needs?

After asking yourself these questions for about two weeks, whenever you go out to eat, you'll begin assimilating the answers without thinking consciously about the questions.

Select Restaurants Carefully

It's easier to order healthfully if you choose dining establishments that offer oil-free pastas, fresh salads and vegetables, salt-free soups, grilled foods made with polyunsaturated oils, bottled waters, and water-processed decaffeinated coffee. Find these restaurants by looking over menus, asking questions, or writing to the American Heart Association. They publish "Dine To Your Heart's Content." It's a free guide put out by the AHA affiliates in almost every state. These guides indicate restaurants, where you live and travel, willing to make changes on request to accommodate your low-cholesterol, low-fat, low-calorie, or low-salt needs.

Now you need the following ordering tips to keep you on track no matter what type of restaurant you're in.

The ABCs of Ordering

A. Think in terms of tradeoffs; for example, choose between an appetizer or dessert.

B. Order a couple of side dishes or an appetizer, in place of an entrée, if you're not too hungry.

C. If you order a glass of wine or a cocktail, request a glass of mineral water at the same time and alternate sips.

D. Avoid sugary, caffeinated soft drinks.

E. Order your salad dressing and all sauces on the side, so you're in charge of how much you use.

F. If you can't find what you want on the menu, ask the waiter if the chef makes any items that are more healthful or ***nutrient dense***—high in nutrients (vitamins and minerals) while low in fat and calories.

Nutrient Density

Nutrient density is a way to evaluate the nutritional quality of foods by comparing the amounts of nutrition they provide against the number of calories they contain. Fruits and vegetables, for example, are nutrient-dense foods because they contain few calories and ample nutrients. In other words, nutrient-dense foods are usually less refined foods. When you start eating more foods as nature intended them, an amazing thing happens—you begin appreciating more subtle flavors.

There are occasional times, of course, when you cannot eat nutrient-dense foods, or you don't want to. Fortunately, you don't need to eat perfectly all the time to stay healthy, assuming your circumstances don't dictate a strict diet. No matter what your specific nutritional concerns are, it's important to know you don't need a different diet for each nutritionally related medical condition—all areas of nutrition work together. The "right diet" to lose weight, gain weight, maintain your best weight plus optimal health, lower your cholesterol, alleviate constipation or high blood pressure, regulate diabetes, and prevent heart disease and many forms of cancer is the same diet healthy people follow to stay that way. Just make sure the mainstay of your diet consists of complex carbohydrates (fruits, vegetables, and grains), low-fat dairy products, and sufficient lean protein. It's that simple.

So, why does the subject of nutrition seem confusing, particularly when it comes to ordering in restaurants? Nutrition is a new science, and it's usually presented in a confusing way.

Guidelines put out by major institutions are generally described in unfamiliar vocabulary, equivalents, and percentages that are hard to convert into menu choices. (For example, Cholesterol: 100 milligrams/1,000 calories; maximum of 300 milligrams/day. Saturated fat: 10 percent of calories. Total fat: 25 to 30 percent of calories. Carbohydrate: 50 percent of calories; increase emphasis on complex varieties. Sodium: 1 gram per 1,000 calories; maximum of 3 grams per day.) It's easy to get confused.

Unless you have a computer with one of the better nutritional software programs and the time and energy to tabulate everything you eat and drink daily, it is difficult to know what percentage of your diet comes from fat, carbohydrates, and protein.

Wouldn't it be nice if we didn't have to be mathematicians or statisticians to understand the terminology and figure out the relationship between good nutrition and good health? We could simply walk into restaurants and order high-fiber, low-salt, delicious meals containing less than 30 percent fat, no simple sugar, and moderate-size portions. That's exactly how health-conscious people want to order, and to accommodate their needs more restaurateurs are writing their menus with that in mind.

Although on most menus good-tasting healthful dishes are still hard to find, while unhealthful foods are readily available, once you know what you should be eating, there is every reason to get what you want in every type of restaurant. With a little bit of planning—the 12-Step Dining Out Program—you can stay on your eating plan while eating in any restaurant.

Chapter 3

▲

THE 12-STEP DINING OUT PROGRAM

WITH the 12-Step Dining Out Program you can follow any eating plan. These dietary guidelines for healthy people are a combination of recommendations made by the U.S. Department of Health and Human Services, U.S Department of Agriculture, American Heart Association, The Surgeon General's Report on Nutrition and Health, National Cancer Institute, and American Dietetic Association.

Just remember to check with your doctor before starting this nutritional plan, because your individual circumstances determine to what degree you should adhere to each of these dietary health principles.

▲

STEP 1

MAINTAIN A WEIGHT THAT IS HEALTHY FOR YOU

Determine whether or not you need to lose weight, using these three methods:

- Look at yourself in a full-length mirror. Sometimes we don't see ourselves accurately, however, so double-check your perceptions with the two methods that follow.
- Compare yourself with people you know, not movie stars, similar to you in age and height who look good and emulate them.
- Check the following height/weight range chart to find out approximately how much you should weigh.

Weight Range Chart

Men

Height *Feet*	*Inches*	*Small Frame*	*Medium Frame*	*Large Frame*
5	2	128–134	131–141	138–150
5	3	130–136	133–143	140–153
5	4	132–138	135–145	142–156
5	5	134–140	137–148	144–160
5	6	136–142	139–151	146–164
5	7	138–145	142–154	149–168
5	8	140–148	145–157	152–172
5	9	142–151	148–160	155–176
5	10	144–154	151–163	158–180
5	11	146–157	154–166	161–184
6	0	149–160	157–170	164–188
6	1	152–164	160–174	168–192
6	2	155–168	164–178	172–197
6	3	158–172	167–182	176–202
6	4	162–176	171–187	181–207

Women

Height Feet	Inches	*Small Frame*	*Medium Frame*	*Large Frame*
4	10	102–111	109–121	118–131
4	11	103–113	111–123	120–134
5	0	104–115	113–126	122–137
5	1	106–118	115–129	125–140
5	2	108–121	118–132	128–143
5	3	111–124	121–135	131–147
5	4	114–127	124–138	134–151
5	5	117–130	127–141	137–155
5	6	120–133	130–144	140–159
5	7	123–136	133–147	143–163
5	8	126–139	136–150	146–167
5	9	129–142	139–153	149–170
5	10	132–145	142–156	152–173
5	11	135–148	145–159	155–176
6	0	138–151	148–162	158–179

Weights at ages 25–59 based on lowest mortality. Weights in pounds according to frame (in indoor clothing weighing 5 lbs. for men and 3 lbs. for women; shoes with 1" heels).

Courtesy Metropolitan Life Insurance Company

How Much to Lose

If you need to lose weight, determine how much.

1. Write down how much you weigh. _____
2. Write down your goal weight. _____
3. Subtract those two numbers. _____
4. The difference equals the number of pounds you need to lose. You need to gain if you weigh less than your goal weight. (Eat healthful snacks daily in addition to your regular meals.)

How Many Calories to Eat a Day

Find your activity level and sex on the following chart. It determines the formula you need to calculate the number of calories you should eat a day. If you need to lose, multiply the number in parentheses times your goal weight. If you want to maintain your weight, multiply the number in parentheses times your current weight, for your daily calorie allotment.

If you exercise or work hard physically two to three times a week, or more, you are active. Anything less is considered inactive.

Active Women	=	(12) × (goal) or (current weight).
Inactive	=	(10) × (goal) or (current weight).
Women	=	(15) × (goal) or (current weight).
Active Men	=	(13) × (goal) or (current weight).
Inactive Men		

Not "Just a Salad" is based on the slow but sure approach to weight loss and good health, because it takes a long time to lose weight without losing your health. Two to three days are required to eliminate, from your eating plan, the 3,500 calories it takes to lose a pound without depriving yourself of the nutrients you need to maintain good health.

The average man must take in approximately 1,800 daily calories to obtain the nutrients he needs. The average woman needs 1,200 daily calories to obtain the vitamins and minerals she needs. Therefore, unless you're extremely overweight, it's impossible for your weight to plummet while obtaining the nutrients you require. It helps to know that weight is not lost a whole pound at a time. When the scale shows a quarter-or half-pound loss, that's progress, and you have reason to rejoice.

Just be certain to take in the nutrients you need, because if you restrict your caloric intake drastically problems arise. Your body acts as though it's starving and slows down your metabolism (the rate at which you burn calories) to conserve as much energy as possible, and instead of losing fat you'll begin breaking down lean muscle tissue. What's the point of being thin if you don't have good health? The following ten tips will help you stay trim while maintaining your health.

Weight Loss Tips

- Eat three nutritious meals a day. Most important, please don't skip breakfast. (The breakfast foods I recommend are listed in chapter 5.)
- Keep a food diary. Write down everything you eat and drink. Indicate the time of day, or night, what's going on at the time, and how much you eat. If you regain a few pounds, you can analyze your diary to find out why.
- If you feel hungrier than usual on a particular day, enjoy a healthful snack such as an apple, for 80 calories. Eat it an hour or two before going out to eat. It takes the edge off your appetite. Avoid eating sugary or salted snack foods. Other healthful snack ideas are listed in chapter 5.
- Avoid products containing artificial sweeteners, including sugarless gum and diet sodas. They may create the desire to eat sweets.
- Reduce your salt intake. Too much salt causes weight gain from water retention. Lemon juice, vinegar, herbs, and spices are good salt substitutes.
- Drink purified water daily. Water is the only calorie-free nutrient. It quenches your thirst, fills you up, nourishes your skin, and helps eliminate waste products. The amount of water needed varies from person to person, but four to six 8-ounce glasses is a good standard to follow. If you can tolerate that much, drink an 8-ounce glass of hot or cold water when you get up in the morning and then another one every few hours until 8:00 P.M. Following this advice is difficult, but if you

drink a lot of water, your weight loss results will amaze you.

- Step up your exercise program with the consent of your physician. Exercise that gradually increases your heart rate, and keeps it there at least twenty minutes three times a week or more, provides the best conditioning.
- If you drink alcoholic beverages, do so only occasionally and in moderation (12 fluid ounces of beer, or 5 fluid ounces of wine, or 1½ fluid ounces of liquor).
- Don't make chewing gum a habit; it may increase your appetite.
- To cut down on calories, don't snack at night after your evening meal.

▲

STEP 2

EXERCISE DAILY WITH THE CONSENT OF YOUR PHYSICIAN

Choose aerobic activities you enjoy such as walking, tennis, biking, dancing, or swimming. They burn calories without breaking down lean muscle tissue. Regular exercise will improve your overall health, but if you don't have access to a pool, don't decide to swim. Choose a form of exercise you can do on a regular basis.

Exercise burns calories and keeps our muscles toned. Movement means improvement. To lose weight, exercise more and consume less calories. Or, putting it another way, to lose weight you must burn off more calories than you take in. It's simple. Our weight depends upon two factors: how many calories we eat and how many calories we burn.

If, in restaurants, you are served portions that are too large, don't undo the good you did exercising by overeating. Take home the extra food that would make you feel stuffed and uncomfortable, saving it for another meal. Not a midnight snack.

We have been taught that big is better, so people overeat. But sometimes, less is more. Our stomachs are only meant to hold 32 ounces, on the average. I think Oliver Wendell Holmes was right when he said, "Sometimes we eat as if our stomachs belong to someone else."

▲

STEP 3

TWENTY-FIVE TO 30 PERCENT OF YOUR TOTAL CALORIES SHOULD COME FROM FAT

Limit your saturated fat intake to 10 percent, and your dietary cholesterol to no more than 300 milligrams per day. Avoid coconut and palm oils, gravy, sauces, butter, fried foods, and lard. Hold the mayo, cream, half and half, whole milk, whole-milk cheese, egg yolks, and nondairy creamers. Order meats lower in fat, and trim all visible fat from them. Protein is healthful; it's the fat we need to avoid. Choose vegetable sources to obtain some or all of the protein you need.

▲

STEP 4

FIFTY-FIVE TO 65 PERCENT OF YOUR TOTAL CALORIES SHOULD COME FROM COMPLEX-CARBOHYDRATE FOODS

Compared with protein and fat, three times the amount of calories you eat should come from complex carbohydrates—fruits, vegetables, and grains.

▲

STEP 5

INCLUDE FIBER IN YOUR DAILY DIET, PARTICULARLY THOSE COMING FROM FRUITS, VEGETABLES, AND WHOLE GRAINS

Fiber helps prevent colon cancer, lowers cholesterol, aids digestion, and makes you feel full. Complex-carbohydrate foods are rich in fiber, so by eating them regularly you will naturally obtain the fiber you need.

▲

STEP 6

TEN TO 15 PERCENT OF YOUR TOTAL CALORIES SHOULD COME FROM VEGETABLE PROTEIN

Include foods containing protein, other than animal products, such as dry beans, peas, and vegetables in your diet regularly.

▲

STEP 7

EAT A VARIETY OF FOODS IN MODERATION FROM THE MAJOR FOOD GROUPS

The major food groups contain nutrients your body requires on a regular basis, but not necessarily at each meal. Variety and moderation are the keys to a successful eating plan.

The Major Food Groups Renamed

The following examples indicate what constitutes a serving from each group:

1. Bread, Cereals, and Grains: ⅔ cup whole-grain cereals, ½ cup grains (rice, bulgur wheat, kasha), 4 crackers, 1 slice of bread, 2 ounces pasta.
2. Vegetables: One-half cup is equivalent to one serving. Be sure to eat both yellow or orange and green vegetables regularly. Fresh are best. In addition to other nutrients, the yellow and orange varieties such as sweet potatoes, pumpkin, and squash contain vitamin A and beta carotene. Dark leafy greens such as broccoli, spinach, and collard greens contain vitamin B and calcium, in addition to the vitamins mentioned above. Other green vegetables, generally speaking, contain vitamins C and B, except B-12 (found only in animal products).
3. Fruits: One medium-size fruit equals one serving. Eat a variety of fresh fruits regularly. In addition to other nutrients, citrus fruits such as grapefruits, tangerines, and oranges contain vitamin C. Yellow and orange-colored fruits such as apricots, cantaloupe, mangoes, and peaches contain vitamin A and its precursor beta carotene, which may be helpful in preventing cancer.
4. High-Calcium Foods: 8 ounces nonfat and low-fat milk, buttermilk, ½ cup low-fat cottage cheese, ½ cup nonfat and low-fat yogurt, 2 ounces skim-milk cheeses, 3 ounces sardines, ½ cup dark green leafy vegetables.
5. Protein Foods: 6 ounces chicken, turkey (skin removed), fish, low-fat beef, ½ cup peas, dried beans, 4 ounces tofu, 2 egg whites.

Recommended Daily Servings

Eat the recommended number of servings from each of the major food groups daily. Be sure to include five fruits and vegetables a day.

Food Groups	*Servings*	*Foods*
Breads, cereals, grains	6	Rice, bulgur wheat, kasha, crackers, breads, cereals, pasta
Vegetables	3	Squash, broccoli, asparagus
Fruits	2	Grapefruits, oranges, apples, bananas, berries
High-calcium	3	Non-fat and low-fat milk, yogurt, cheeses
Protein, vegetable	1-2	Dried peas, beans, tofu
Protein, animal	1-2	Fish, eggs, meats
Fats, oils, sweets	Use sparingly	Oils, mayonnaise, desserts

▲

STEP 8

LIMIT SALT INTAKE

A safe and adequate amount of salt is 1,100 to 3,300 milligrams per day (2,000 milligrams of salt equal 1 teaspoon). Many foods contain salt naturally, so you can put down the salt shaker and still obtain the amount you need.

▲

STEP 9

USE HONEY AND PROCESSED SUGAR ONLY IN MODERATION

You can enjoy delicious desserts, occasionally, and stay on your eating plan unless your medical circumstances dictate otherwise. It is the butter or fat in most cookies, cakes, and pies that we should avoid. Although sugar and honey are virtually devoid of nutrients, they're not unhealthful when used in moderation.

▲

STEP 10

AVOID FOODS CONTAINING POTENTIALLY UNHEALTHFUL ADDITIVES

Nitrates, sulfites, MSG (monosodium glutamate), pesticides, and unhealthful preservatives, colorings, and flavorings should be avoided. Whenever possible it's best to frequent restaurants that serve poultry, meat, and dairy products that are hormone-free. And, whenever they're available, eat organic produce—fruits and vegetables free of dyes and chemical sprays.

▲

STEP 11

DRINK 4 TO 6 8-OUNCE GLASSES OF WATER DAILY

Although requirements for water may vary from person to person, four to six 8-ounce glasses is a good rule of thumb.

Water will suppress your appetite naturally and help your body metabolize stored fat.

▲

STEP 12

LIMIT YOUR INTAKE OF ALCOHOLIC, CAFFEINATED, AND SUGARY BEVERAGES

Do not drink more than 12 ounces of beer, or 5 ounces of wine, or 1½ ounces of hard liquor a day. During pregnancy, women should not drink alcohol; it increases the risk of birth defects.

THE BOTTOM LINE

Not "Just a Salad" was written in response to what Dr. Sigmund Freud said: "The most powerful urge is to seek pleasure and avoid pain." This principle is a basic motivator; unless the pains of reducing and staying healthy are turned into pleasure, the best-laid plans are worthless because they won't be followed.

With general guidelines for ordering in restaurants and the 12-Step Dining Out Program, you'll stick to your diet because eating out is fun! Now, let's move on to part 2, "Dining Out in Your Favorite Restaurants," for specifics regarding your favorite cuisines.

PART 2

▲

Dining Out in Your Favorite Restaurants

▼

▲

IN today's world it's unrealistic to expect every restaurant item to be healthful. But it is realistic to find at least a few dishes that fit into your eating plan in every type of restaurant, from affordable to expensive.

As you will see in the following chapters, every popular cuisine can be tailored to every special diet if you know which foods to choose and how to have them prepared. In fact, while eating in restaurants, walking through buffet lines, or dining at other people's homes, no one needs to break a weight-loss diet, eat the wrong foods, overeat, or get sick in an attempt to have a good time.

In response to this awareness, I predict that sharp restaurateurs will soon offer such items as organic produce and lean designer beef (hormone- and antibiotic-free) in response to customer demands for more healthful foods. Rather than being disgruntled when requests are given, perceptive waiters will volunteer to meet their customers' special dietary needs. The chefs will then see the specifications on computer terminals in their kitchens and make the appropriate adjustments while cooking.

Menu Command

While technology is playing catch-up with our needs, Menu Command will help you stay on your eating plan. There is a Menu Command in each of the following chapters, related to a different cuisine. Menu Command, the secret to staying on your diet while eating out, tells you which foods to choose and which to avoid. Use it as a guideline since ingredients and cooking methods may vary from restaurant to restaurant.

The dishes "To Choose" will usually fit in with your special dietary requirements because they are low in fat, salt, sugar, and calories while high in fiber and nutrients. Since ethnic dishes are often spelled phonetically, spellings may vary. Just remember, you don't need a different diet for each nutritionally related medical condition.

The dishes "To Avoid" represent unhealthful items that contain too many calories, too much fat, salt, or sugar, and too few nutrients for people concerned with weight loss, high cholesterol, or the prevention of cancer. The reasons a particular dish should be avoided are noted unless they are obvious.

Sample Menus

In addition to Menu Command, you'll find sample menus in each chapter. These menus were selected solely because they are representative of a cuisine. Although most of the menus are from restaurants located throughout southern California, you will find many of the same dishes in your favorite restaurants wherever you live and around the world.

Take *Not "Just a Salad"* with you whenever you go out to eat, or look up a particular cuisine before you get to the restaurant. After a while, you'll know how to convert healthful nutrition principles into smart menu selections without giving it much thought.

Are you ready to discover how to eat out in French restaurants while staying on your diet? In the next chapter you'll see how easy and fun it can be!

Chapter 4

▲

FRENCH FOOD

IF you've ever watched Julia Child cook, you know that most French food is loaded with rich ingredients and topped with creamy and buttery sauces. You may believe it's impossible to diet while dining out in French restaurants. By examining the cuisine, however, you will find that it is possible to eat defensively in French restaurants.

FRENCH REGIONAL COOKING

French cooking is a collection of many tastes and textures, because each region in France has a different cooking style. The region of Normandy, in the northwest of France, has dark green fields covered with apple orchards and grazing cattle. Therefore, beef or veal smothered in sauce, buttered vegetables, and apple pie covered with whipped cream for dessert is a typical restaurant meal in Normandy.

Brittany, on the other hand, has poor soil and is near the Atlantic Ocean, so the Bretons obtain most of their food from the sea. Their fish dishes are simple and lack complicated sauces.

Truffles, or "black diamonds," as they are sometimes called, come from the southwest of France, and since they are rare because no one has found a way to farm truffles, they can be sold for $400 a pound or more. The truffles grow underground, in the shade of trees, and since pigs are able to sniff them out, country women walk these animals in search of them. The pig finds the black diamond, and the woman distracts the pig by sticking an ear of corn in his mouth as she grabs the truffle. Country women use only a few truffles in their cooking so they can sell the rest at their local market.

The southwest of France is also known for its geese. During winter they are put into large earthenware pots to age in their own fat, called *confit*. That's why goose skin gets so crisp when it's cooked. It's delicious, like duck, but unfortunately too fatty for good health.

Chefs from the French Alps also prepare food that is fattening—not because their dishes are made from potatoes that grow in their plains; potatoes aren't fattening. The fat is added when they top the potatoes with butter, cream, and cheese that come from the cows that graze in their rolling meadows. *Pommes de terre au gratin*, potatoes cooked in white sauce, topped with grated cheese, and baked to form a golden crust, is a delicious but fattening dish that originated there.

Most of the entrées in French restaurants are swimming in delicious sauces. We must order these sauces on the side and dip into them sparingly if we want to stay healthy. Fortunately, every French restaurant also has equally delicious healthful dishes to order.

Avoiding Fat

To learn how to order low-fat foods in French restaurants, I suggest that you become a "fat detective." Foods lower in fat are lower in calories, and foods higher in fat are higher in calories. If you eat fat, you get fat. And if you avoid fat, you'll lose weight. It's almost that simple.

The types of fats and oils you consume also matter. *Saturated, monounsaturated*, and *polyunsaturated fats* and *oils* do not contain one type of fat alone. Each contains a combination made up of three types of fatty acids, which because of their chemical makeups affect our bodies differently. For better health, avoid artery-clogging cholesterol and saturated fat. Substitute instead monounsaturated and polyunsaturated oils, which seem to lower the cholesterol in the blood while promoting growth and maintenance of our bodies. Use oils only in moderation, even though they have healthful attributes, since a high-fat diet can lead to overweight and various types of cancer, no matter what types of fats or oils are consumed.

It's easy to identify the different types of fats and oils. Cholesterol, which is mainly a saturated fat, is found only in animal products. Other fats that are hard or firm at room temperature, such as palm and coconut (the tropical oils), are mainly saturated and act like cholesterol in the body. Just by switching from butter or stick margarine to liquid margarine, corn, soy, grape, sunflower seed, or one of the other polyunsaturated oils, food becomes more healthful. (In chapter 5 we'll discuss oils as they relate to foods.)

In French restaurants, I suggest you avoid goose, duck, and the *cassoulet* (made with salt pork, bacon, Polish sausage, duck, and lamb), because they are loaded with saturated fats.

You should also avoid cheese. The French are known for their cheeses, but when it comes to French cheese there is no such thing as "low fat." If you have ever seen melted cheese, you know what I mean. Most cheeses are between 70 percent and 90 percent fat, most of which is saturated. And the creamier the cheese—like *Camembert, Brie*, or *Roquefort*—the fattier.

In restaurants, buffet lines, and other places where you are not in control of the preparation of your food, you need to become observant in order to cut down on the amount of fat you are willing to swallow. Sometimes you can see fat, especially in a sauce, where there are beads of it floating on top. Every mayonnaise-based dish is loaded with fat. In fact, there are 100 calories of fat in 1 tablespoon of mayonnaise.

You can taste fat. Vegetables feel slick in your mouth when they are loaded with butter. Your lips feel slick. Salads look and taste greasy when they are drenched in dressing. So simply by being selective about what you are willing to eat, you can avoid fat. If after tasting a food you realize it is full of fat, push it aside.

But does food still taste good without fat? I assure you that it does. Imagine eating crusty French bread dipped into a piping hot bowl of *bouillabaisse*, loaded with garlic, and staying on your eating plan. Delicious French dishes can be prepared fat-free.

Marge

Whenever I think of French food I think of Marge, an account executive I counseled who works at a prestigious advertising firm. She wanted to lose weight and keep it off, but dining with VIP's was part of her job. She had to eat dinner out every night, most of the time in fancy French restaurants here and abroad.

Marge began ordering fish or chicken, poached or steamed. Occasionally she'd enjoy beef roasted or grilled. She'd also order a salad, thick white asparagus (89 calories for 3 ounces), an artichoke (hot or cold), or little red potatoes (rolled in fresh herbs). Eating this way she had lost twenty-one pounds and three inches from her hips, within three months.

"Sure, I've had to give up alcohol, cookies, candies, and gooey desserts," she explained, "but because of the benefits, I don't feel deprived."

Like Marge, you'll find there's something wonderful about going into a restaurant where the mood is right, ordering low-fat high-fiber foods, feeling in charge, and having great-looking, delicious-tasting, low-calorie food placed in front of you.

▲

La Tour—A Typical French Restaurant

The menu that follows from the Chicago restaurant *La Tour*, is similar to many French menus. Let's look at it to see how one can eat French food out regularly, maintain a balanced diet, and still lose weight.

Although the majority of the dishes on the menu are prepared with heavy cream, butter, and cheese, **I have placed checkmarks next to the dishes that you can choose without going off your diet.**

Cold Appetizers

Napoleon of Smoked Salmon with Fresh Melon and Double Cream

*Ballottine of Fresh Seafood with Lemon Chervil and Smoked Crab

√ Fresh Lobster Salad with Papaya, Yogurt and Lime

Terrines and Pâtes of La Tour

Caviar Available Upon Request

Soups

Clam Bisque with Basil and Red Pepper Coulis

Chilled Cream of Avocado with Grilled Florida Shrimp

*Consommé of Seafood with Saffron and Truffles

Hot Appetizers

Confit of Duck with Smoked Cabbage and Mushrooms

Gratin of Goat Cheese with a Black Olive Puree, Tomato and Basil Fondue

√*Carpaccio of Marinated Tuna with a Petite Salad, Fresh Horseradish Sauce

Ravioli of Artichokes, Shrimp and Fresh Dill
with a Shallot and Snail Compote

Salads

√Mixed Greens

√La Tour Salad with Mustard Vinaigrette

√ Tomato and Red Onion with Watercress, Basil Vinaigrette

√Bibb Lettuce with Radicchio and Belgian Endive, Lemon and Chive Vinaigrette

√Italian Frisśee with Goat Cheese and Sweet Garlic Vinaigrette

Fish and Seafood

√*Braised Salmon with Wild Mushrooms, Crayfish Broth and Leeks (Request oil, not butter, be used)

√*Grilled Swordfish Steak with a Ragôut of Endives, Pearl Onions and Artichokes

Saufeed Red Snapper Ĉote d'Azur with Olive Croustade

√Opera of Braised Seafood with Watercress, Cucumbers and Ginger (Request oil, not butter, be used)

√Combination of Saufeed Florida Shrimp and Sea Scallops with Garden Vegetables and a Chive Vinaigrette

Entŕees

*Steamed Breast of Pheasant with Leeks and Asparagus, Truffle Sauce

Medallions of Veal with Peppered Tomatoes and Watercress Cream Sauce

Saufeed Veal Kidneys with Mustard and Black Pepper

Saufeed Sweetbreads and Wild Mushrooms with Brandy and Peppercorns

Saufeed Breast of Duck with Honey and Vinegar and Fresh Chives

Game and Fowl of the Season

From the Broiler

√*Broiled Breast of Chicken with Apples and Shallots

Filet Mignon of Beef with Bone Marrow and Bordelaise Sauce

√=**Recommended**

New York Strip Steak and Braised Onion and Herbs
Broiled Lamb Chops with Grilled Eggplant, Endive and Tomato Sauce
*Suggested Low-Calorie Dishes

Cut Calories

By ordering items prepared without butter and cream, you can save an entire day's allotment of calories (see table below). Multiply that over a week's time and you can lose two pounds a week, or eight pounds a month. If you appreciate the nuances of French cuisine—the way French waiters pace a meal and how their timing allows for relaxation—that's exciting news.

Average Meal	*Better Choices*	*Calories Saved*
Napoleon of smoked salmon with fresh melon and double cream *Approx. calories = 525*	Fresh lobster salad with papaya, yogurt and lime *Approx. calories = 250*	*275*
Clam bisque with basil and red pepper *coulis* *Approx. calories = 325*	Tomato and red onion with watercress, basil vinaigrette *Approx. calories = 125*	*200*
Gratin of goat cheese with a black olive puree, tomato and basil *fondue* *Approx. calories = 285*	*(Don't order every course)*	*285*
Sautéed breast of duck with honey and vinegar and fresh chives *Approx. calories = 625*	Grilled swordfish steak with a *ragout* of endives, pearl onions, and artichokes *Approx. calories = 250*	*375*
Total Calories Average meal = 1,760	Total Calories Better Choices = 625	
	TOTAL CALORIES SAVED = 1,135	

Diners often look at a menu and feel they should order à la carte items in every category imaginable, including hot and cold appetizers, but you don't have to order a dish from every group. You may prefer three appetizers, soup, salad, and coffee for your meal.

Although French restaurateurs are responding to the public's plea for lower-fat and -calorie foods by preparing more grilled fish, roasted chicken, and an abundance of barely cooked vegetables, don't down an oversize dessert to reward yourself for "ordering right." Choose one that's low in fat, and you'll feel good about yourself in the morning!

If, however, a chocolate *éclair* or any other high-calorie dessert looks too good to pass up—and you must succumb—split it with a friend, eat it slowly, and enjoy every morsel. Then go back to your eating plan right away. And remember, it's what you eat most of the time that matters most.

✓To Choose

These items will enable you to stay on your eating plan while eating out in French restaurants. They are lower in fat, salt, sugar, and calories than the items to avoid.

Drinks (Boissons)

Cidre doux (sparkling apple cider)
Citron pressé (fresh-squeezed lemon juice with water): add a little sugar, diet permitting
Eau d'Evian (Evian water)
Eau minérale (mineral water)
Perrier (mineral water)
Schwepps (in France tonic water is called "Schwepps"; a Schwepps contains sugar, but less salt than other sodas)

Choose **Perrier or Evian. If you want to drink alcohol in moderation, order a wine spritzer—half club soda or Perrier and half wine.**
BEST BETS: **Perrier, Schwepps, or (diet permitting) wine spritzer**

Appetizers (Hors d'Oeuvres)

Artichauts vinaigrette (artichokes vinaigrette)
Coquilles Saint-Jacques (scallops in wine sauce)
Fresh lobster with papaya or melon
Huîtres à la vapeur avec citron (steamed oysters with lemon)
Poireaux vinaigrette (leeks vinaigrette)
Purée de poisson (puree of fish)

Choose **fish, seafood, poultry, beef, and vegetable appetizers.**

✓ To Choose

***BEST BET:* Artichauts vinaigrette**

Soups (Potages)

Bouillabaisse (shellfish soup from Marseilles): a meal in itself
Bouillon blanc de veau (white beef broth)
Bouillon blanc de volaille (white chicken broth)
Bouillon de poisson (fish broth)
Consommé (clear beef broth)
Potage de tomates (fresh tomato soup)
Potage Saint-Germain (fresh pea soup): order if made without ham
Soup du jour (soup of the day): find out what it is and order if it's not salty, oily, or creamy

***Choose* vegetable, pureed, or tomato-based soups.**
***BEST BET:* Potage Saint-Germain**

Bread (Pain)

Pain français (French bread): sourdough or regular

***Choose* regular or sourdough French bread.**
They contain 140 calories for a two-inch slice and very little oil.
***BEST BET:* French bread**

Salads and Vegetables (Salades et Légumes)

Asperges en branches (whole boiled asparagus)
Macédoine de légumes (carrots, peas, green beans)
Pommes de terre à la vapeur (steamed potatoes)
Ratatouille (eggplant, squash, and bell pepper compote)
Salade de champignons (mushroom salad)

✓To Choose

Salade de tourteaux (crab salad): order with vinaigrette and hold the mayo
Salade Niçoise (lettuce, hard-boiled egg, potatoes, string beans, anchovies): order the dressing on the side—it's a meal
Salade verte à la vinaigrette (green salad with French dressing)

***Choose* a dark green lettuce, such as romaine (they contain more nutrients than head lettuce). Remember to order your salad dressing on the side.**
BEST BETS: Salade Niçoise* or *asperges en branches

Entrées (Plat Principal)

Bar poché (poached bass)
Brochette de boeuf (brochette of beef)
Brochette de poulet (brochette of chicken)
Brochette de veau (brochette of veal)
Coq au vin (chicken in wine sauce): when made with oil and no salt pork
Filet de poisson pochés au vin blanc (fish poached in white wine)
Filet de veau (fillet of veal)
Filet mignon au jus (filet mignon in its own juice): 3½ ounces equals one serving
Lapin à la moutarde (rabbit in mustard): without the skin, rabbit is relatively lean
Lapin au vin rouge (rabbit in red wine sauce): without the ham
Moules à la Marinière (mussels mariner's style)
Poissons aux câpres (fish fillets with capers)
Pot au feu (steamed beef stew)
Poulet au citron (lemon chicken)

✓To Choose

Poulet au pot (chicken in the pot): delicious on a cold, rainy day
Poulet aux fines herbes (roast chicken with herbs)
Saumon poché (poached salmon)
Steak au poivre (pepper steak)
Turban de sole (fish mousse): a good substitute for pâté
Viande de veau (veal meat): order if lean

***Choose* dry-broiled, poached, or steamed dishes.**
BEST BETS: poulet au citron* or *saumon poché

Sauces (Assaisonnement)

Sauce ravigote (made with oil, herbs, and garlic)
Sauce tomate (tomato sauce): with herbs, garlic, and onion

***Choose* oil and garlic or tomato-based sauces.**
BEST BET: Sauce tomate

Desserts (Desserts)

Compote de pruneaux (stewed plum compote)
Decaf/café au lait (decaffeinated coffee with steamed milk): ask for nonfat milk, close your eyes and think of this as dessert
Ile flotante: poached meringue
Pêches au vin (peaches in white wine)
Pomme au four (baked apple): delicious topped with nonfat milk
Raspberries, blueberries, or strawberries
Salade de fruits (fresh fruit salad)
Sorbet aux fruits (fruit sorbet—lemon, orange, strawberry, green apple, and so on)
Your leftover French roll

✓To Choose

Choose **desserts that don't contain a lot of fat or sugar.**
BEST BETS: Pomme au four**, fresh fruit sorbet, with a cup of nonfat decaf/*****café au lait*****.**

⊘To Avoid

Drinks

Armagnac
Cognac
Cointreau
Grand Marnier
Marc and other after-dinner drinks

Avoid **sweet and creamy after-dinner drinks.**
They are higher in calories, ounce for ounce, than other alcoholic beverages. And if they're accompanied by a coffee drink made with whipped cream and sugar, you may end up with as many calories as you consumed eating the main course. So, no *café au lait* with cognac.

Appetizers

Caviar (fish eggs): generally salty and oily
Cervelles (brains): too high in cholesterol
Duck: too fatty
Escargot (snails): fatty
Fromage fondue (cheese dip)
Kidney: high in cholesterol
Pâté (a combination of meats): too fatty
Ris de veau (sweetbreads): all organ meats are high in cholesterol
Saucissons (cold dry sausage appetizers)

⊘To Avoid

***Avoid* foods that are buttered, creamed, sautéed, or fried.**

Breads

Croissants (prebuttered rolls): one croissant contains 200 calories

***Avoid* bread and rolls that have been made with butter, egg yolks, shortening, or lard.**

Soups

Cream of asparagus, potato, or broccoli
Soupe à l'oignon (onion soup with cheese and croutons)
Velouté laitue (cream of lettuce soup)

***Avoid* all soups made with cream, butter, or cheese.**

Salads and Vegetables

Haricots verts à la crème (green beans in cream)
Pommes de terre Anna (mold of sliced potatoes in butter)
Salade Russe (Russian salad): loaded with mayonnaise
Salade verte au roquefort (green salad with *Roquefort* cheese): the dressing is loaded with mayonnaise and sour cream

***Avoid* salads with *Roquefort* and mayonnaise-based dressings. One tablespoon contains 225 calories.**

Entrées

Andouillette grillée (grilled sausage)
Boeuf bourguignon (beef in a red Burgundy wine sauce made with salt pork)

⊘To Avoid

Boudin (sausage)
Canard (duck)
Cassoulet (white bean stew with sausage, goose, chicken, or pork)
Côtelettes de veau (veal chop)
Crevettes à la crème (shrimps in cream)
Cuisses de grenouilles (frogs' legs)
Foie de veau (calf's liver made in butter): liver is high in cholesterol
Foie gras (goose liver)
Foies de volailles (chicken livers)
Homard thermidor (lobster casserole made with butter and cream)
Langue de boeuf (tongue)
Oie Farcie (goose)
Ossobuco (veal shanks made with vegetables)
Pieds de cochon (pig's feet)
Quenelles (a puree of fish bound together with an egg-and-cream sauce)
Quiche Lorraine (ham, cheese, and vegetable pie): loaded with cream
Sole à la Normande (contains heavy cream)

***Avoid* dishes that are creamed, *au gratin*, or scalloped.**

Sauces

Coulis (concentrated tomato sauce): loaded with cream
Mayonnaise (made with egg yolk and oil)
Sauce béarnaise (made with butter and egg yolks)
Sauce béchamel (made with milk and butter)
Sauce espagnole (classic brown sauce containing butter, red wine, and flour)
Sauce Hollandaise (made with butter and egg yolk)

⊘TO AVOID

Sauce madère (like sauce espagnole with additional butter)
Sauce mornay (contains butter, light cream, and Swiss cheese)
Sauce mousseline (like Hollandaise with heavy cream)
Sauce velouté (made with butter, chicken broth, and egg yolk)

***Avoid* French sauces loaded with butter, cream, egg yolk, and cheese.**

Desserts

Cerises flambées (flambéed cherries)
Cheese plate (may contain more fat than your entire meal)
Choux à la crème (cream puffs): contains cream and eggs
Crème caramel (caramel custard)
Crêpes Suzettes (thin pancakes with sauce): contains flour, milk, eggs, a little oil, butter, and liquor
Fraises Romanoff (strawberries Romanoff)
Gâteau au chocolat (chocolate cake)
Grand Marnier soufflé (puffy cake with egg yolk, butter, flour, and Grand Marnier)
Mille feuilles (Napoleons, French puff pastry with chocolate cream filling)
Mousse au chocolat (chocolate mousse)
Pêche Melba (peach Melba)
Petits pots de crème au chocolat (chocolate cream custard)
Profiteroles au chocolat (cream puffs and chocolate sauce)
Tourte au fromage (cheesecake)

***Avoid* French pastries and cakes made with egg yolk, butter, and cream.**

Customized Dishes

What should you do if you're in a French restaurant where the menu doesn't list the items Menu Command suggests?

First, decide what you feel like eating, how you want it prepared, and then ask for it. Remember, the French pride themselves on freshly prepared food. So it's easy for French chefs to customize dishes to your diet, if they want to.

Convincing a classic French chef to push aside fat-laden sauces made with butter, cream, eggs, and cheese for the dictates of ***cuisine minceur*** (cuisine of slimness) can be tricky, but certainly not impossible.

Talented chefs know how to substitute healthy ingredients for unhealthy ones and create delicious dishes that are good for us by using an abundance of fresh vegetables, fruit, pasta, and other complex carbohydrates to make what I call healthful cooking. Sauces can be made without cream or butter. Pureed vegetables such as cauliflower or red, green, and yellow bell peppers are used to make sauces for pasta and fish dishes. French chefs are advocates of simplicity when they want to be. They'll avoid using butter and use reduced stock and lots of fresh herbs instead.

As long as you don't overeat, you can leave any French restaurant feeling light and healthy, not heavy. So explain your nutritional needs to your waiter, and most French chefs will prepare foods according to your needs.

French Defensive Dining Tips

Here are four tips for anyone who wants to stay on a diet while eating out in a French restaurant:

1. Ask for your salad dressing on the side. Take a spoonful of dressing from the bottom of the terrine, obtaining as many of the herbs as possible. Then pour the oil off the top. The dressing that remains on your spoon is the most flavorful part. This technique works because oil rises. Using this process, sprinkle up to four "lower in oil" teaspoons of dressing on your salad.

2. Choose foods mesquite-grilled, dry-broiled, poached, steamed, or *en papillote*—wrapped in foil, sprinkled with oil and herbs, and baked in the oven or grilled over charcoal.
3. Order entrées made with red or white wine rather than cream sauces.
4. Always request oil instead of butter in the preparation of your food.

FRENCH PHRASES

The following phrases make it possible to order healthful meals when the menu is in French and the waiters don't speak English. You can choose the appropriate sentences and show them to your waiter. Or, if you are brave, read them aloud even if you don't speak French.

1. **I want my food made without butter and cream. Please bring all sauces on the side.**
   J'aimerais un plat cuisine sans beurre ni crème. S'il y a une sauce, apportez la moi à part, s'il vous plaît.

2. **I would like a green salad with vinaigrette dressing (on the side).**
   J'aimerais une salade verte avec une vinaigrette. (Apportez-moi la vinaigrette.)

3. **Please bring me lean beef, chicken, fish, or turkey (choose one of the following cooking methods):**
   a. Mesquite-grilled
   b. Dry-broiled

c. Poached

d. Steamed

e. Wrapped in foil, sprinkled with oil and herbs, and baked in the oven.

S'il vous plaît apportez-moi du boeuf degraissé, du poulet, du poisson, ou de la dinde (choisissez un de ces méthodes de cuisson):

a. Cuit(e) au charbon de bois

b. Grillé(e)

c. Poché(e)

d. Cuit(e) à la vapeur

e. En papillote, humecté d'un peu d'huile, saupoudré d'herbes, et cuit(e) au four.

4. I would like a fresh green or yellow vegetable prepared without butter or sauce.
J'aimerais des légumes verts préparés sans beurre ni sauce.

5. Please bring me a basket of French bread.
J'aimerais un peu de pain français, s'il vous plaît.

6. I'd like a bowl of soup prepared without cream.
J'aimerais de la soupe fait sans crème.

7. Please bring me a cup of coffee (decaffeinated) with nonfat milk and fresh fruit for dessert.
Apportez-moi, s'il vous plaît, une tasse de café (décaféiné) avec du lait écrémeuse et des fruits frais comme dessert.

8. All I need is the check, thank you.
Je veux l'addition, s'il vous plaît, merci.

THE BOTTOM LINE

More and more restaurants in the United States and in Europe are changing their menus to satisfy a calorie-counting, nutrition-conscious clientele. French food can be incorporated into a healthy diet if you start out with lower-calorie items and have them prepared simply, without added fat and sauces.

Buttered, creamed, in cream sauce, *au fromage*, and fried are clues—on the menu—that tell you what to avoid. Order your dishes dry—that is, without butter, mayonnaise, or any other added fat. Request sauces and dressings on the side so you can decide how much to use. Oil and fat have more than twice the calories—ounce for ounce—than fruit, vegetables, and grains.

It's easy to stick to your eating plan, even in French restaurants, once you've made up your mind.

As we've seen, cutting down on fat is the best way to cut calories and lose weight in French restaurants and, as you'll see in the next chapter, in American restaurants, too.

Bon appétit! (Enjoy yourself!)

Chapter 5

▲

AMERICAN FOOD

IF you're like most people, you'd enjoy eating a chili burger on a fresh onion roll, with thick slices of tomato and Bermuda onion and lots of mustard or ketchup; but since you've learned that red meat is linked to a high cholesterol level, you think twice.

Cholesterol is not our only concern, however. The typical American diet has led to increased incidences of heart disease, cancer of the colon, breast, and prostate, high blood pressure, osteoporosis, diabetes, constipation, and obesity.

Fortunately, as evidence links a healthful diet to the prevention of disease, many Americans are more interested in ordering smart, but not everyone has made the transition to a low-fat diet. Fat constitutes 37 to 40 percent of the total calories Americans eat. Only about 40 percent of the typical American diet comes from complex carbohydrates (fruits, vegetables, and grains), instead of the desired 55 to 65 percent. And, because of an overabundance of processed foods, the American diet contains too much sugar and salt.

Before we can dine defensively in American restaurants, we need to take a look at what American food is besides the traditional hamburger, which, by the way, you don't have to give up.

American Regional Cooking

In addition to hot dogs, thick soups, salads, meat loaf, mashed potatoes, and apple pie, American food is an amalgamation of dishes created from ingredients available in the various regions throughout the United States.

The Indians, America's native inhabitants, cooked dishes that usually contained corn. Their recipes became classics after being passed on from generation to generation. Settlers who first arrived in New England began cooking with foods from both the land and sea and formulated dishes such as New England clam chowder and Boston baked beans.

Maryland crab cakes, sweet potato pie, and country-style greens were made with ingredients originally available only in the South such as collard greens, okra, and yams. Rib-sticking comfort foods, on the other hand, originated in the Midwest.

From Louisiana, Creole and Cajun dishes are created from local ingredients from the bayou, sea, and farms, which give them their distinctively spicy tastes and smoky flavors. And Texas, New Mexico, and Arizona lend a southwestern influence to dishes throughout the United States, using ingredients such as avocados, cilantro, tomatillos, jalapeño peppers, and fresh limes.

Finally, chefs from the Pacific states—Alaska, Washington, Oregon, California, and Hawaii—use the wealth of fresh seafoods, fruits, and vegetables from their geographical extremes to rethink the food traditions of many cultures. With great flexibility and creativity, California chefs are able to transform every cuisine into a healthful culinary experience.

THE WAR ON FAT

Fat is the biggest nutritional problem in the American diet today. Butter, lard, or coconut oil are added to foods such as crackers, chips, gravies, breads, and desserts. To help prevent many forms of cancer, heart disease, and obesity, the American Heart Association and other health groups have recommended calories coming from fat should make up no more than 30 percent of a person's total caloric intake.

But before we talk about how to cut down on the amount of fat in your diet, please fill out the following questionnaire.

How Much Fat Is In Your Diet?	*Your Answers*
1. How many times a week do you eat in fast-food restaurants?	______
2. Do you request low-fat cooking methods in restaurants?	______
3. How many times a week do you eat deep-fried foods such as fish, chicken, vegetables, or potato chips?	______
4. Do you, your parents, brothers, or sisters have coronary artery disease or cancer?	______
5. How many servings of cream, half and half, whole-milk yogurt, ice cream, cheese, or nondairy creamer (made with coconut oil) do you consume each week?	______
6. Do you request nonfat milk and other nonfat dairy products in restaurants?	______

7. How many servings (3½ ounces) of beef, chicken, fish, turkey, veal, or pork do you eat a week? __________

8. Do you generally order low-fat meats and remove all visible skin and fat? __________

9. Do you order all sauces, dressings, and gravies on the side? __________

10. How many times a week do you eat coldwater fish such as herring, mackerel, salmon, sardines, lake trout, tuna, or whitefish? __________

11. Do you eat desserts regularly? __________

12. How many pats of butter or margarine do you use a week? __________

13. Have you tried using Butter Buds instead of butter? __________

14. Do you ask for soy, safflower, corn, canola (Puritan), olive oil, or Pam in the preparation of your food instead of butter or margarine? __________

15. How many egg yolks do you eat a week? __________

Now I'd like you to evaluate your answers by reading the following discussion. The numbers preceding each paragraph correspond with the questionnaire.

Cut the Fat

1. Although many ingredients used in American fast-food establishments are fat-free, some dishes become unhealthful when fat is added during the cooking process. Eliminate some of the fat in your diet by ordering more healthful lunches and dinners—made without fat—and you'll have a good chance of losing weight, lowering your blood cholesterol level, while enjoying American food in restaurants. Depending upon what you order, fast food can be a healthful or unhealthful supplement to your diet.

2–3. Look for dishes on fast-food American menus and in fine dining establishments that are mesquite-grilled, cooked in broth, in a tomato base, or in their own juice, dry-broiled, grilled, baked in the oven, poached, roasted, or steamed. Steer clear of all foods that are braised, buttered, cooked in butter sauce, creamed, cooked in cream sauce, fried, crispy, pan-fried, or scalloped.

4–10. If you have a family history of coronary artery disease, don't use whole-milk products. Request nonfat dairy products instead. Order dishes that incorporate animal protein as a condiment rather than as the main course. Trim all visible fat from your meat and take the skin off poultry. Order sauces, dressings, and gravies on the side so you're in control of how much you use. And eat plenty of fish, especially deep-sea, cold-water fish such as tuna, salmon, and sardines because their omega-3 fatty acids may help prevent heart disease.

11. Fortunately, sugar isn't as unhealthful as we're led to believe. It's the butter or fat in most cookies, cakes, and pies that we should avoid. Unless you have diabetes or hypoglycemia, you can enjoy delicious desserts once in a while without going off your diet if you choose those without a lot of fat.

Saturated Fat

12. I recommend that you avoid butter and margarine (unless it's the liquid type) because both contain *hydrogenated*—a fancy name for saturated—fats. They're high in calories, too. In fact, one tablespoon of butter, one little pat, contains 100 calories. Depending upon the brand, margarine contains between 50 and 100 calories. Unfortunately, in most American restaurants bread and butter are placed at each table at the beginning of a meal, so buttering bread becomes a habit, especially when eating out. If you can't resist the butter, ask the waiter to remove it from your table. Bread tastes delicious plain, especially when you keep in mind that nothing tastes as good as it feels to be healthy!

13. If you must have a replacement for butter, Butter Buds is a healthy substitute that can be carried into any restaurant.

Polyunsaturated Oils

14. To lower the saturated fat content of every American meal, ask the chef to cook your food with the healthful *polyunsaturated* oils such as soy, safflower, sunflower, grape, corn, or canola. Canola has the lowest percentage of saturated fat of all oil products on the market. But use even this oil in moderation, because all oils are caloric. Pam, a polyunsaturated vegetable oil cooking spray, is another healthful alternative to butter or margarine.

15. Recently I saw a woman in a coffee shop take a can of Pam from her purse and hand it to the waitress, requesting that the chef use it in the preparation of her three-egg-white, one-yolk omelet. (Since one egg yolk contains 213 milligrams of cholesterol and the American Heart Association recommends a maximum of 300 milligrams of dietary cholesterol per day for healthy adults, she was smart.) When her meal arrived,

I asked her how she liked it. She answered that although it didn't look as pretty as a three-egg-yolk omelet made with butter, it tasted just as good.

So remember, if you order scrambled eggs or an omelet, request that the chef throw away one or more of the yolks and cook with one of the more healthful oils instead of butter to cut down on cholesterol.

Monounsaturated Oils

On your salads and in the preparation of your food, olive, peanut, canola, and other *monounsaturated* oils are the best to request, because studies show they lower the harmful LDL (low-density lipoprotein) cholesterol while keeping the helpful HDL (high-density lipoprotein) cholesterol levels constant. Most restaurants have olive oil, lemon juice, and Dijon mustard on hand. Mix them together, right at your table, and you'll have a delicious-tasting dressing.

CHOLESTEROL

Cholesterol is a fatlike substance present in every living cell in the body. Too much blood cholesterol narrows and finally clogs our arteries. Narrowed arteries prevent our blood from flowing freely, and that can cause a heart attack or stroke.

Cholesterol, however, is not a bad thing except when you have more than you need. It helps maintain good health, produces bile, which aids in the digestion of fats, allows for proper growth, and helps produce hormones.

Cholesterol is carried through the bloodstream to its destinations in one of two primary forms of cholesterol, called *lipoproteins. LDL* (low-density lipoprotein) is damaging when there's too much. *HDL* (high-density lipoprotein) is beneficial when there is a lot, because it is a scavenger that gets rid of the harmful LDL cholesterol.

How high is your cholesterol level? Check with your doctor if you don't know. If your level is above 240, and you have risk factors such as a family history of heart disease, you smoke, don't exercise, and eat a fatty diet, you are at high risk of having a heart attack. If your level is below 200, you have a desirable level and less to worry about, at least in this department. And if your level is between 201 and 239, it is considered borderline high, which means you are at moderate risk of having heart disease. These numbers are particularly significant if your HDL is less than 35. Check with your physician, and begin to lower your cholesterol to a desirable level by changing your diet.

Three factors determine the amount of cholesterol in our blood:

- the amount we take in from the foods we eat
- how much we manufacture in our bodies
- how efficiently we use cholesterol

We have no control over how much cholesterol we manufacture, or use, because that's determined by factors beyond our control. We do have control over what we eat, however. Let's take charge!

Foods That Lower Cholesterol

Even if your cholesterol level is below 200, I recommend that you eat a high-soluble-fiber cereal for breakfast regularly to stay healthy. Soluble fiber absorbs the bile acids in the bowel, preventing it from producing cholesterol. Oat and rice bran are good examples, so restaurateurs interested in offering delicious, healthful foods to their customers are using them to make cereal and muffins.

Look for a high-fiber cereal on the menu of your local coffee shop. Or take a box of the hot cereal you like most and ask if they'll make it for you regularly. Enjoy your favorite cereal with a bagel or toast and fresh fruit—grapefruit, cantaloupe, stewed prunes, raisins, or a banana. A breakfast like this is much better for you than eating the traditional bacon and eggs, sugary cereals, syrup-drenched waffles with ham, or butter-fried French toast.

If you need to lower your cholesterol level, you may want to use the following Low-Cholesterol Guide. It lists foods to eat (such as popcorn and mayonnaise made with safflower oil, vinegar, and no egg yolk) that will help you cope with your low-fat future. Most people can lower their cholesterol level with simple, sensible changes in their eating habits without having to take medications. But remember, consult with your physician before beginning any new nutritional regimen.

Low-Cholesterol Guide

Major Food Groups	*Use*	*Avoid*
1. *Calcium Foods*	Nonfat, skim milk, powdered skim milk, low-fat cottage cheese (in moderation), nonfat yogurt (regular and frozen)	Ice cream, cream, half and half, whole milk, regular cheese, cream cheese, nondairy creamers, tofutti
2a. *Protein: Animal* (4 to 6 oz. daily)	Chicken, turkey (skin removed), shellfish, fish, lean beef, and veal	Lamb, ham, bacon, skin from poultry, fish-oil supplements, marbled, fatty meats, sausages, luncheon meats, organ meats (liver, kidney, brain, and tongue)
	Egg whites, egg substitutes	Egg yolks
2b. *Protein: Vegetable*	Dried beans, peas, tofu	Nuts

Major Food Groups	*Use*	*Avoid*
3. *Fruits and Vegetables*	All fruits, all vegetables, popcorn, air-popped or made with a healthful oil	Fried foods
4. *Breads, Cereals, and Grains*	*High-fiber cereals:* Wheatena, oatmeal, cream of wheat, Nutri-Grain, Grape-Nuts, shredded wheat, Kölln, and Health Valley cereals	All cereals, crackers, breads, pastries containing lard, butter, stick margarine, coconut, palm, and hydrogenated vegetable oils
	Crackers: Finn Crisp, rice crackers, Ideal, and Kavli Flat Bread	Egg matzos
	Breads: Sourdough, pita, Pritikin breads, tortillas, chapati, English muffins, water bagels, bialys, waffles, pancakes	Egg bagels
	Grains: Bulgur wheat, polenta, pasta, rice, kasha, kashi, couscous	Egg noodles
5. *Fats*	Sunflower seed, corn, soy, safflower, grape oil, canola oil, olive oil	Butter, stick margarine, coconut, palm, hydrogenated vegetable oils, lard, beef tallow, and saturated fats in salad dressings, sauces, and gravies
	Butter Buds, Pam, safflower egg-free, fat-free mayonnaise	Mayonnaise

Exercise

To win the battle of the bulge, there is more to consider than careful ordering in restaurants. It is important to exercise daily. Exercise strengthens the heart and blood vessels, lowers high blood pressure, helps regulate high blood sugar, burns fat, tones the body, and raises your HDL. It also increases the density of your bones and improves the flexibility of your joints. But always be sure to consult your doctor before beginning any new exercise program.

Some of the best exercises are those that don't require a lot of equipment, such as low-impact aerobic classes or walking. A brisk walk is particularly good before and after eating, because it speeds up your metabolism.

A client of mine reported parking his car three-quarters of a mile away from the restaurants where he dines to get some exercise at the end of the day. As an added bonus he saved valet parking expenses.

Calories Burned While Exercising

- Low-impact aerobics (for one hour) burns 260 calories.
- Strolling leisurely (1 or 2 MPH) for one mile will burn 100 to 120 calories.
- Functional walking (2 to 4 MPH) for one mile will burn 120 to 140 calories.
- Brisk or fitness walking (3.5 to 5.5 MPH) can raise the pulse, produce an aerobic effect, and burn 120 to 160 calories per mile.

How to Eat a Healthy American Diet

Eggs

If your cholesterol level is above 240, I suggest you limit your consumption of eggs to no more than one per week, because they are high in cholesterol. It's only the yolk, however, that contains cholesterol, so have as many egg whites as you want. Egg white omelets are delicious. Raw eggs may contain salmonella, however, so only eat eggs that have been fully cooked.

Buffets

Some American restaurants are known for their all-you-can-eat buffets. Before deciding what to eat from a buffet, walk through the line to see what's available.

Choose foods that look freshly made, healthful, and delicious while avoiding buttery, greasy, mayonnaise-based, fat-laden dishes. Use several plates instead of piling lots of items together until everything blends and tastes alike. If a dish you selected doesn't taste good, or is fattier, saltier, or more sugary than you expected, don't eat it. You can always go back and get more food if you're still hungry.

Those Tricky Salad Bars

Many clients ask what they should eat for lunch. Salad can be a good choice, if you choose carefully. Waldorf, pasta, potato, and ambrosia salads are loaded with hidden fat because of the cream, cheese, luncheon meats, and mayonnaise that are added.

When you want a salad, I suggest you select fresh greens, sprouts, tomatoes, and mushrooms that don't contain many calories—rather than items marinated in oil—topped with crabmeat, flaked tuna, chickpeas, kidney beans, and a low-calorie dressing mixed with additional vinegar or lemon juice.

Salad and dressing can be more caloric than a three-course

meal. One serving (four tablespoons) of regular Italian dressing contains 332 calories, Thousand Island dressing 320 calories, and French dressing 264 calories. Beware of caesar dressings made with raw egg; they may contain salmonella.

Remember this trick to cutting calories from your salad dressing: Take a spoonful of dressing and pour most of the oil off the top; the remaining dressing in the spoon is the most flavorful part because it contains most of the herbs and spices, so you don't need to use too much.

Fresh fruit is available at most salad bars. A large plate of melons and berries or mixed fruit makes a light lunch.

When you don't feel like eating salad, enjoy a white meat turkey or tuna sandwich on a kaiser roll or French bread, with lettuce, tomato, and a little mustard or safflower mayonnaise. The white meat contains less fat than the dark, and kaiser rolls and French breads are usually made with the more healthful types of oils.

Fish

You should eat fish often. All deep-sea, coldwater fish and some species that live in cold fresh water such as herring, mackerel, tuna, salmon, and sardines—rich in the omega-3 fatty acids—have been linked to the prevention of heart disease. Since grilled fish, a fish sandwich, or salad are available in most American restaurants, eating fish often is easy.

Shellfish

New evidence reveals that you can eat moderate amounts of shellfish, six ounces twice a month, while lowering your cholesterol level. People who have high blood levels of cholesterol were generally told not to eat shrimp, lobster, and crab, but now we know they can eat these foods in moderation, because the saturated fat and cholesterol content of shellfish is considerably lower than once thought. It takes, in fact, two dozen jumbo shrimp to match the cholesterol in one egg yolk. Mussels, oysters, and scallops are also low in cholesterol, but since these foods are reputed to carry disease when raw, eat them only when they're cooked.

Lean Beef

What about those burgers I said you can eat? You can have a lean hamburger or turkey burger—not the greasy fast-food type—once in a while. The issue is not whether to eat lean steak or ground beef, but how much of it to eat. The average person can have six ounces of lean protein throughout the day, or they can enjoy it all at one meal.

If you miss the red meat you've taken out of your diet, you'll be happy to know that there's more cholesterol in fatty meat than lean varieties. From a health standpoint, beef graded "select" is better than more expensive "choice" or "prime" cuts because fewer of its calories come from fat. Lean beef contains no more cholesterol, ounce for ounce, than chicken, even roasted chicken without the skin.

The best way to get the fat out of your meat (and keep some money in your pocket) while still enjoying a good piece of beef occasionally, is to order the leaner, yet delicious, select cuts such as flank, sirloin, eye of round, round tip, top loin, top round, and tenderloin. Ask the waiter which dishes contain lean beef. Instead of all-you-can-eat prime rib dinners, many restaurants are now offering smaller portions of lean beef.

Beef received bad publicity because it was so fatty. But today cattle are bred and fed differently. Designer beef gives us meat with less hormones, fat, cholesterol, and calories. Beef packs protein, B vitamins, and many essential minerals, such as heme iron, which is more absorbable than other types. Lean beef contains a lot of nutrition for its calories. In fact, three ounces of lean meat now has just 192 calories. Beef contains slightly more protein, ounce for ounce, than chicken.

So you can eat a lean burger occasionally without concern. Just be sure to balance out the rest of the day by including cholesterol-free foods such as dried beans, egg whites, and vegetables to obtain more of the protein you need without the fat.

Order Everything Feasible on the Side

I suggest making "on the side, please" your new motto at restaurants for everything feasible—especially gravies, sauces, and dressings. That way you can decide whether or not to use them.

At An American Place, off Park Avenue in Manhattan, your gastronomic needs will be accommodated.

▲

AN AMERICAN PLACE MENU

Appetizers

✓ Chilled Marinated Seafood and Shellfish Salad
with a roasted lobster vinaigrette
✓ Field Salad of Baby Lettuces and Seasonal Greens
California olive oil vinaigrette
and a country wheat goat cheese crouton
Smoked Free Range Chicken and Lentil Soup
with autumn greens
✓ California Endive, Romaine and Red Oak Leaf Salad
with caesar dressing and shaved aged cheese
[Request vinaigrette on the side]
Brochette of Spicy Lamb and Apple Sausage
with a Hoppin John salad and a red wine vinaigrette
Oysters on the Half Shell
with fresh horseradish mignonettes

Main Courses

✓ Herb Roasted Breast of Chicken with Cabernet Whipped Potatoes
with an herb pan gravy
[Request the gravy on the side]

√ Sauteed Maine Red Shrimp with Sticky Rice Timbale
and with a spicy ovendried tomato vinaigrette
√ Fresh Pasta with Stewed Chicken and White Beans
and fresh basil oil
√ Cedar Planked Atlantic Salmon with Winter Squash
apple cider vinegar sauce
√ Grilled Barbecued Yellow Fin Tuna
country style wild rice and hottish BBQ sauce
Grilled Boneless Loin of Pork
with carmelized N.Y. State apples
red onions and a natural sauce
Warm Hudson Valley Camembert Crisp
with an Old Fasioned Waldorf Salad
upland cress and toasted pumpkin seed vinaigrette
Cripsy Buffalo Style Chicken Salad
with a creamy Iowa blue cheese dressing
Chesapeake Bay Deviled Crabcakes with Straw Potatoes
mustard herb dressing
Old Fashion Hollywood Brown Derby Cobb Salad
roasted chicken breast, avocado, bacon, tomato, hard-boiled egg, lettuces, watercress and crumbled blue cheese freshly tossed with derby dressing
[substitute chicken for the bacon and omit cheese]

Desserts

Double Chocolate Pudding
Banana Betty
Old Fashioned Chocolate Devil's Food Cake
Angel Food Chiffon
with raspberry sauce
Warm Fresh Fruit Crisp
with vanilla cream
Coconut Creme Caramel
with tropical fruit ambrosia
Old Fashioned Fresh Berry Shortcake
with farm fresh whipped cream
[Omit the whipped cream]
Homemade Peanut Butter Ice Cream Sandwich
with chocolate cookie wafers and "chips"

Homemade Ice Cream

Beverages

Coffee	Cappuccino	Espresso	Tea

Decaffeinated Available

▼

AMERICAN FAST FOOD

In a twenty-four-hour period it's not easy to juggle work, exercise, family, fun, and food. In trying to handle so many aspects of life, you can run out of time, drop one of those "balls," and neglect a proper diet.

The National Restaurant Association reports that one out of five Americans, 45 million people, eat in a fast-food restaurant on any given day. If you frequent fast-food restaurants, it's best to avoid hot dogs and other smoke-cured meats. They usually contain nitrates in addition to more than the recommended 30 percent fat. Nitrates and nitrites that can form nitrosamines have been linked to cancer of the stomach.

You can eat burgers, as I promised, but it's best not to eat the fast-food types often. Unfortunately, as the following table shows, over 30 percent of the calories in Burger King, McDonald's, Wendy's, and Jack-in-the-Box burgers—including meat, bun, dressing, cheese, and garnishes—come from fat. If you eat these burgers, reduce the fat by special-requesting yours without the "special sauce" or mayo, bacon, and cheese—to save 200 calories. Then, balance out your total calories coming from fat by choosing foods lower in fat during the remainder of the day. It's your total diet that counts, so it's what you eat most of the time that matters.

Because of consumer demands, the heads of the major fast-food chains are now considering nutrition, rather than taste alone, when deciding what to use in their products and how to cook their food. Some chains are grilling lower-fat burgers

Restaurant	*Item*	*Calories*	*% Calories from Fat*
Burger King	Hamburger	275	39
	Whopper	626	55
	Whopper with cheese	709	57
McDonald's	Hamburger	263	33
	Big Mac	560	52
	Quarter Pounder with cheese	520	51
	McLean	320	28
Wendy's	Hamburger	350	46
	Cheeseburger	580	53
Jack-in-the-Box	Cheeseburger	323	41
	Jumbo Jack with cheese	630	50

rather than frying them, and they are switching to less saturated fats to cook their fries. So, even though a large order of French fries still contains approximately 400 calories, fast-food fries just got better.

Fast-food spots are making other improvements, too, offering their patrons breakfast cereals, fat-free muffins, salad bars, prepackaged salads, lower-fat shakes, skinless chicken, low-fat frozen yogurt, and 1 percent low-fat milk. Healthful fast-food items and restaurants are available. I've even ordered healthful food alternatives at Disneyland, Disney World, and Dodger Stadium!

✓To Choose

Other American fast-food restaurants offer chicken and fish to promote a healthful image, but beware because even when the skin has been removed, these items are generally breaded and then deep-fried. If you take the skin off chicken and scrape the tartar sauce off a fish sandwich, you'll save a third of the calories and almost two-thirds of the fat.

But you don't have to rely on fast-food establishments to obtain healthful and fast American food. You can turn any one of your favorite restaurants into a fast-food establishment by calling ahead. That way a healthful meal will be ready, to eat in or take out, when you are.

Use the American Menu Command to increase the amount of fiber you eat while trimming cholesterol, fat, oil, salt, sugar, and calories from your diet.

Drinks

Club soda
Coffee: in moderation
Fresh juice
Herbal teas
Mineral waters (plain or with fruit essence)
Nonfat milk
Seltzer water
Soft drinks (fructose-based and decaffeinated are best)

***Choose* drinks without too much sugar, caffeine, or fat.**
***BEST BETS:* Mineral waters, club sodas, and seltzer water**

Appetizers

Barbecued oysters with cocktail sauce
Cantaloupe

✓TO CHOOSE

Crab Louie (flaked crabmeat, cayenne pepper, grated onion, chili sauce piled high)
Gefilte fish: if your diet permits salt
Shrimp cocktail with cocktail sauce

***Choose* appetizers that aren't too salty, creamy, or greasy.**
***BEST BET:* Shrimp cocktail with cocktail sauce**

Soups

Barley beef and vegetable
Beef and vegetable
Borscht (beet soup)
Cioppino (fisherman's stew)
Lentil
Manhattan clam chowder
Split pea
Tomato
Turkey rice
Vegetable

***Choose* soups that are made with defatted chicken or beef broth and no cream.**
***BEST BETS:* Cioppino (fisherman's stew), vegetable soup**

Breads

Alaska sourdough bread
Bagels (plain or onion)
Bialy (bagellike bread made without oil)
Boston brown bread
Lavash (Armenian cracker bread)
Pancakes (without butter)

✓To Choose

San Francisco sourdough French bread
Waffles (without butter)

***Choose* breads made with polyunsaturated oil.**
***BEST BET:* French bread**

Vegetable Dishes

Artichoke
Asparagus
Baked potato
Boiled potatoes
Broccoli
Butternut squash
Cherry tomatoes
Cobb salad: substitute more turkey for the ham
Creole slaw (contains no mayonnaise)
Mixed vegetables vinaigrette
New potatoes roasted with lemon, chives
Okra in tomato sauce
Oven-roasted potatoes
Oven-roasted potato skins
Peas with onions
Spaghetti squash
Stir-fried vegetables
String beans in tomato sauce
Succotash (corn, lima beans, and green beans)
Vegetable kabobs

***Choose* fresh vegetables that are baked, steamed, or sautéed in a little oil.**
***BEST BETS:* Artichoke, baked potato, or stir-fried vegetables**

✓TO CHOOSE

Bean, Pasta, and Rice Dishes

Brown rice
Pasta with summer vegetables
Three-bean salad
White rice
Wild rice

***Choose* bean, pasta, and rice dishes that aren't made with a lot of oil.**
***BEST BETS:* Brown rice or pasta with summer vegetables**

Poultry

Barbecued chicken
Barbecued turkey
Chicken burger
Chicken gumbo (a stew made with chicken, seafood, rice, peppers, and tomatoes)
Club sandwich: hold the bacon and mayo, of course
Curried chicken
Roast chicken: remove the skin
Roast Rock Cornish hen: remove the skin
Roast turkey: remove the skin
Turkey burger

***BEST BETS:* Roast chicken or turkey burger**

Fish

Abalone
Broiled Atlantic scrod
Broiled fresh tuna
Broiled Hawaiian halibut steak with lemon and dill

✓To Choose

Broiled swordfish
Fillet of sole
Grilled albacore
Grilled salmon
Lobster (boiled, broiled, or steamed)
Louisiana boiled seafood dinner: delicious hot or cold
Mesquite-grilled mackerel
Mesquite-grilled sand dabs
Oven-steamed sea bass
Poached salmon steak with marinated cucumber
San Francisco seafood casserole (shellfish and whitefish mixed with clam juice, tomatoes, and white wine)
Stir-fried scallops
Trout
Whitefish

***Choose* fresh fish that has been baked, broiled, or steamed.**
***BEST BETS:* Salmon steak, tuna, or mackerel**

Meats

Bison (low in fat)
Brisket of beef: if it's lean
Buffalo (low in fat)
Burgoo (a Southern stew whose main ingredients are lean beef, potatoes, okra, corn, tomatoes, and beans)
Eye of round
Filet mignon
Flank steak
Hamburger: if it's lean
London broil
Meat loaf: if it's lean

✓To Choose

New York steak
Pork: if it's lean
Round tip
Sirloin
Swiss steak
Tenderloin
Top loin
Top round
Yankee pot roast (boneless chuck, potatoes, carrots, small white onions, and parsley)

***Choose* lean meat that is roasted, broiled, grilled, barbecued, or simmered in its own juices.**
***BEST BETS:* Eye of round or flank steak**

Spreads, Dressings, and Sauces

Apple butter
Cocktail sauce: use only in moderation, diet permitting sugar
Horseradish
Jams, jellies: diet permitting, low-sugar varieties are best
Mustard: diet permitting salt
Ketchup: moderation is the key, diet permitting sugar
Maple syrup: moderation is the key
Peanut butter: contains oil, so eat in moderation
Salsa cruda (vegetables simmered in tomato sauce)
Salsa roja
Salsa verde

***Choose* spreads, dressings, and sauces without added fats or oils. Use them in moderate amounts.**
***BEST BETS:* Apple butter and low-sugar spreads**

✓TO CHOOSE

Desserts

Angel food cake (an extremely light cake that became popular in the twenties)
Applesauce: without added sugar
Fresh fruits
Frozen yogurt: nonfat varieties
Gelatin: if your diet permits sugar
Strawberry shortcake: hold the whipped cream

***Choose* desserts low in sugar and fat.**
***BEST BETS:* Angel food cake or fresh fruit**

⊘TO AVOID

Drinks

Alcoholic beverages
Eggnog
Hot chocolate
Irish coffee (contains whiskey)
Soft drinks (containing sugar or caffeine)
Whole milk

***Avoid* alcoholic beverages and drinks containing caffeine, fat, or an abundance of sugar.**

Appetizers

Clam fritters (chopped clams in egg batter and deep-fried)
Corn oysters (corn combined with egg and fried in butter)
Oysters Rockefeller (an oyster topped with butter, spinach, celery, and green onion and baked)
Rumaki (contains bacon and liver)

⊘TO AVOID

Avoid **fatty appetizers.**

Soups

Chicken noodle (usually contains chicken fat and egg noodles)
Corn chowder (contains milk and cheese)
Cream of celery
Cream of chicken
Cream of mushroom
Cream of tomato
Cream of watercress
Creamy California artichoke
Lentil and frankfurter
Lobster bisque (contains cream)
Matzo ball (contains egg yolk and chicken fat)
New England clam chowder (contains butter, cream, and sometimes salt pork)
Onion soup gratiné
Pumpkin bisque (contains cream)

Avoid **creamy, salty soups.**

Breads

Bread stuffings: they usually contain butter
Buttery biscuits
Cornbread
Croutons: they are usually soaked in oil and add unnecessary calories
Egg bagels
Johnnycake (fried cornmeal disk)
Parker House rolls: contains flour, butter, sugar, and salt
Southern cornbread: contains sugar and shortening

⊘ To Avoid

***Avoid* breads made with sugar or saturated fats.**

Vegetable Dishes

Buttered lima beans
Caesar salad (torn romaine lettuce with dressing of anchovies, oil, and lemon juice, a coddled egg, and Parmesan cheese): eliminate most of the croutons
Cajun home-fried potatoes
Candied sweet potatoes
Coleslaw: contains mayonnaise
Corn fritters
Corn pudding: contains whole milk, eggs, and cream
Country-style greens: contains bacon or lard
Creamed onions
Cucumbers in sour cream
French fries
Fried onion rings
Glazed carrots: contains butter and sugar
Hash brown potatoes
Hominy cakes (simmered hulled white corn mixed with butter and fried into cakes)
Hush puppies (cornmeal and water mixed together and fried in bacon grease; originally used to hush howling hounds)
Mashed potatoes: contains whole milk and butter
Pan-fried new potatoes with rosemary
Pickles: too salty
Potatoes au gratin: contains cheese
Potato latkes (fried potato pancakes)
Potato salad: contains mayonnaise
Scalloped potatoes
Spinach, mushroom, and bacon salad
Sweet potatoes

⊘ TO AVOID

Twice baked potatoes: contains butter and cheddar cheese
Waldorf salad

***Avoid* salads and vegetables that contain added fat.**

Bean, Pasta, and Rice Dishes

Boston baked beans: contains brown sugar and salt pork
Fettuccine with cream
Macaroni and cheese: contains butter, milk, and cheese

***Avoid* side dishes that contain added sugar and fats.**

Poultry

Chicken à la king (patty shells filled with cooked chicken in cream sauce)
Chicken Andouille jambalaya (one-pot meal with sausage)
Chicken croquettes
Chicken potpie
Chicken tetrazzini (chicken, mushrooms, and pasta in cream sauce)
Goose: too fatty
Old-fashioned creamed turkey with biscuits
Quail: too fatty
Southern-fried chicken (chicken parts coated with seasoned flour and then fried)

***Avoid* chicken that contains added fat.**

Fish

Fried catfish
Jambalaya: contains shrimp, ham, and sausage

⊘ To Avoid

Lobster Newburg: contains butter and cream
Lox: contains nitrates
Louisiana seafood fry
Maryland crab cakes: contains mayonnaise
Pan-fried trout
Seafood filé gumbo: contains sausage
Seafood fry
Shrimp scampi (shrimp sautéed in garlic and butter)
Soft-shelled crabs (sea crabs dipped in flour, sautéed in butter)
Tuna noodle casserole: contains whole milk or cream

***Avoid* fish dishes that contain added fat.**

Meat

Beef stew: usually made too salty and fatty in restaurants
Chicken-fried steak with cream gravy
Corned-beef hash: contains butter and nitrates
Country-fried steak
Ham: contains nitrates
Hot dogs: contain nitrates and too much fat
Lamb: too fatty
Liver: contains too much cholesterol
New England boiled dinner (corned beef, vegetables, potatoes): the beef contains nitrates
Porterhouse steak
Prime rib
Short ribs
Spareribs
Standing rib roast
T-bone steak
Texas chili
Veal chop: too fatty

⊘TO AVOID

Avoid **meats marbled with fat.**

Spreads, Dressings, and Sauces

American-style turkey gravy
Blue cheese dressing
Cream cheese
Cream gravy
Creole sauce (made with tasso—Cajun "seasoning meat" that contains pork)
Mayonnaise: "Hold the mayo" is definitely the way to go
Russian dressing (mayonnaise, tomato puree, chopped gerkins, parsley, and sweet pepper)
Sour cream
Tartar sauce: contains mayonnaise
Texas-style barbecue sauce: usually contains butter and sugar
Thousand Island dressing (ketchup and mayonnaise combined)
Wildberry syrup: too much sugar

Avoid **sauces that contain sugar and fat.**

Desserts

Apple brown Betty
Apple crisp
Apple pandowdy (similar to apple pie)
Baked Alaska (sponge cake piled high with ice cream and covered with meringue)
Boston cream pie
Bread pudding
Brownies
Bundt cake
Cheesecake

⊘To Avoid

Chocolate-chip cookies
Chocolate layer cake
Chocolate pudding
Coffee cake
Cupcakes
Deep-dish apple pie
Doughnuts
Fruitcake
Fruit pies: there's butter in the crust
Fruit cobbler
Giant popovers (a batter without leavening baked in custard cups)
Gingerbread: contains shortening and brown sugar
Ice cream
Joe froggers (spicy molasses cookies, popular since colonial times)
Key lime pie (lime juice, eggs, sugar, and condensed milk inside a pastry shell)
Lady fingers
Lemon meringue pie
Mincemeat pie
Mississippi mud cake
Mousse
New Orleans beignets (deep-fried pastry balls sprinkled with sugar)
Pecan pie
Pralines
Rice pudding: contains whole milk, sugar, and cream
Sour cream sugar cookies
Sticky buns (pecan cinnamon rolls)
Tapioca pudding

***Avoid* sugary, fatty desserts.**

American Defensive Dining Tips

These eleven tips will help you avoid fat, lose weight (if you need to), and stay on a healthful eating plan when eating American food.

1. Pick your restaurants wisely.
2. Limit the amount of coffee and alcohol you drink.
3. Don't allow long periods to elapse without eating. That way you will not overorder or overeat.
4. Depending upon your appetite, order two or three items per meal.
5. Split one entrée and two soups or salads with a friend.
6. Order entrées made with defatted chicken, beef broth, or wine rather than cream sauces.
7. Avoid dishes that use cheese as a main ingredient.
8. Request canola or olive oil instead of butter in the preparation of your food.
9. Order gravies, salad dressings, and sauces on the side.
10. Order nonfat yogurt, strawberry shortcake without whipped cream, or fresh fruit for dessert instead of gooey pastries.
11. Avoid all-you-can-eat diners. Although they're inexpensive, they cost a lot in calories.

American Phrases

Here are ten suggestions you can tell your waiter when it seems there's nothing appropriate on the menu.

1. **I'd like a basket of hot French bread. No butter, thanks.**

2. **Please bring me a tossed green salad with olive oil, Dijon mustard, and fresh lemon on the side. Thanks.**

3. **I'd like a bowl of homemade soup if it was made without cream or salt.**

4. **Please bring me a serving of your freshest fish broiled without butter.**

5. **I would like skinless white meat chicken broiled with lemon and herbs.**

6. **I'd like a six-ounce broiled or grilled lean hamburger, and hold the sauce.**

7. **I'd like a three-egg omelet cooked in oil instead of butter, and please ask the chef to toss out two of the yolks. Thanks.**

8. **I'd like a plate of fresh, seasonal vegetables steamed without butter.**

9. **Please bring me a baked potato with salsa and chives on the side.**

10. **For dessert I'd like a baked apple or a bowl of fresh berries.**

The Bottom Line

When it comes to the American diet, the message, from the American Heart Association to the U.S. surgeon general to the National Cancer Institute, is clear: "*Eat less fat!*"

Whenever possible avoid dishes containing butter, stick margarine, lard, beef tallow, and saturated vegetable oils such as coconut, palm kernel, and palm oils.

When you do eat fats, choose polyunsaturated or preferably monounsaturated vegetable oils (olive and canola) rather than the unhealthful saturated ones. All fats should be used sparingly, however, because they are twice as high in calories as carbohydrates and proteins. This takes determination, but it can be done.

The way chefs are willing to accommodate their customers is refreshing. Now, let's see what we can do to get the fat out of Italian meals, too. Eat out often and enjoy yourselves, my friends!

Chapter 6

▲

ITALIAN FOOD

ITALIAN food is becoming the most frequently ordered and best liked of all ethnic cuisines in the United States. Not long ago, if you wanted a healthful Italian meal you had to settle for a salad or a cup of vegetable soup, because starchy foods used in Italian dishes—such as beans, rice, potatoes, and bread—were thought to be fattening.

Now, health-conscious patrons are adding these delicious complex-carbohydrate foods to their healthful eating plans as they're discovering that starches provide energy. *Pasta* tastes better when it's not swimming in oil, and *pizza* is more delicious when it's not drowning in cheese.

Regional Italian Cooking

In Italy there are twenty-two cooking styles, one from each of its twenty-two regions. Until 1861 Italy was not united, so each region had different rulers, separate armies, and distinct approaches to food. Even today there is no such thing as typical Italian cooking.

People in each of Italy's twenty-two regions also have their own way of speaking. The more dialects a country has, the more cooking styles it has developed. In the United States people have accents, not dialects. Californians understand New Yorkers, and similar foods are served across the country. The same dishes are recognizable from Portland, Oregon, to Portland, Maine. But in Italy you won't find the same authentic dishes on restaurant menus in Venice, Palermo, or Naples, even though all three of these Italian cities specialize in seafood.

From region to region each cuisine varies depending upon the ingredients available to the chefs in each district. Cattle are raised in the mountains of the northern Italian regions, so meat and dairy products are readily available there. In southern Italy meat, butter, and cream are usually not available. The people are poorer, and because they don't eat out as often as the people from the north, southern Italian chefs create satisfying, healthful meals such as *pizza* and *lasagne* using basic ingredients in one dish.

Lombardy, Emilia-Romagna, Tuscany, Rome-Lazio, and Sicily are the regions of Italy most known for their food.

Lombardy

Milanese cooking, which is often colored with saffron, originated in Lombardy. Legend has it that the use of saffron began when a painter put it in the *risotto* (Italian rice) that was going to be served at his daughter's wedding party so gold would reach the tables of the poor people.

Ossobuco originated just outside of Milan and is now famous internationally. The Milanese also invented *panettone*, a bread-like cake that is on every Italian family's table at Christmastime.

Emilia-Romagna

Tortellini (small round twists of pasta filled with meat or cheese) are one of the most popular products from Emilia-Romagna. *Ragù* (a rich sauce made with beef, vegetables, butter, and cream) also came from there. Emilia-Romagna is known for its excellent sausages, called *salame da sugo*, which find their way into almost every dish in Bologna. That's why this town has been called *La Grassa*, or "the Fat One."

Tuscany

Because Tuscany is located midway between the north and south, it is Italy's gastronomic meeting ground. Tuscany is known for its delicious bread and grilled foods. There, butter and olive oil are used in equal proportions in dishes requiring fat. In other words, elaborate gravies and sauces are not used to disguise the flavor of food. Although the task of the Tuscan cook is not easy, the results are savory and healthful.

Rome-Lazio

There are more restaurants in Rome than in any other city in Italy, and their produce is the best, thanks to the mineral content of the soil. The artichokes, beans, celery, lettuces, and peas are exceptionally delicious. Artichokes stuffed with bread crumbs, parsley, and anchovies, *carciofi alla romana* (steamed artichokes), or *carciofi alla giudia* (fried artichokes) are typically Roman. A famous pasta dish, *spaghetti all' amatriciana*, also originated there. Unfortunately, it's laced with bacon and *pecorino* (an extremely fatty cheese), so this delectable dish doesn't fit in with a healthful diet.

Sicily

Sicily is an island off Italy's southern shore, so Sicilians eat a lot of fish. The sea provides not only octopus and squid, but anchovies, eel, sardines, sea bass, sole, and tuna. Eggplant and zucchini are abundant in Sicily, so these vegetables often accompany their meals. *Pizza* is quite popular in Sicily. Sicilian deep-dish *pizza*, unlike *pizza* in all other places, is probably the most delicious pie in the world.

ITALIAN REGIONAL MEAL

When a typical meal is served in Italy, no matter which region you are in, one appetizing dish follows another—there is no main course. An *antipasto* usually precedes the soup. *Antipasto* means "before the meal." It is savored slowly to stimulate the production of gastric juices for the courses to follow.

To cut down on the amount of fat in the *antipasto*, I recommend you eat the vegetables and avoid the *Italian Genoa* (salami), so you can enjoy traditional Italian appetizers while staying on your healthful eating plan.

Zuppa (soup) is sometimes served next, but if it contains *macaroni* or beans, a *pasta* dish is never served at the same meal.

If no soup is served, or if it is a clear one, *pasta* or *gnocchi* dumplings filled with potatoes is the next course.

When *pasta* or *gnocchi* isn't served, *risotto* (Italian rice) or *polenta* (cornmeal porridge) is often ordered instead. *Polenta* can be freshly made, as *pizza di polenta* (cornmeal pie), grilled and covered with tomato sauce or flavored with vegetables. It's delicious.

Rice is served as frequently as *pasta* in Italian restaurants, because more rice is produced in Italy than anywhere else in Europe. Italians generally combine rice with fish, chicken, meat, or vegetables, but they never serve it as an accompaniment to the main dish.

Italians generally follow their first course (*primi*) with a meat, chicken, or fish dish (*secondi*). If vegetables weren't served as an *antipasto*, they are usually served next, and then a salad often follows. Each dish is served one after the other.

In Italy, the cheese and fruit course comes last; dessert is usually eaten only at celebrations. Italians love good food, but even with all these delicious dishes, they don't like to overeat. They also frown on intoxication, so hard liquor or after-dinner drinks are seldom consumed. ***Vino*** (wine), ***un Campari-soda*** (Campari and soda), ***un americano*** (Campari and red vermouth), or ***una birra italiana*** (Italian beer) are more popular.

Italian Restaurants in America

The appetizer is often forgotten during an Italian meal in America. Soup and salad are usually the first courses. Then fish, chicken, or meat is served—generally with a vegetable and potato—as the entrée. *Pasta* is often served alone. Dessert and coffee usually end the meal.

In the United States, Italian food is generally talked about in terms of northern and southern Italian cooking. And the ingredients that are used to cook northern and southern Italian foods are based upon what the earth and sea produce in the northernmost and southernmost areas of Italy. The key to eating out healthfully in Italian restaurants in the United States is finding the lighter southern items on the menu and knowing how to modify the northern-style dishes. The chart that follows shows the similarities and differences.

Italian dishes don't have to be oozing with butter, creamy sauces, and melted high-fat cheeses to be enjoyable. *Pasta, pizza*, beans, bread, meat, and potatoes can be turned into healthful, delicious foods if you have the chef prepare them with lots of garlic, tomato sauce, and low-fat cheese instead.

In Italian restaurants order red sauces, which contain less fat and fewer calories than the white ones. If you stop eating

Northern Versus Southern Italian Food

North	*South*
Antipasti Foods requiring preparation, such as stuffed mushrooms, pickled eggs, or *caponata* (eggplant appetizers), are preferred.	*Antipasti* The south goes in for more olives, celery, carrots, hot peppers, and vegetables.
Starches When *pasta* is eaten, egg *pasta* (*pasta all' uova*) is the favorite form. Rice dishes and *polenta* (cornmeal mush) are also dominant.	*Starches* Tubular-shaped *pasta*—dried flat noodles made without eggs—are commonly used. *Lasagne* and *pizza* are popular.
Fats Butter is the chosen cooking fat, but olive oil is also used.	*Fats* Olive oil is used instead of butter.
Seasonings In the north, *cacciatora* dishes contain rosemary, anchovies, vinegar, garlic, herbs, and butter or olive oil. Tomatoes are seldom used.	*Seasonings* *Cacciatora* in the south contains tomato sauce. Tomatoes are often used.
Garlic is preferred in the north.	Onions are preferred in the south.

pasta all' Alfredo—pasta with a white, thick, creamy, buttery sauce poured on top—and start eating your *pasta* with marinara sauce—fresh tomatoes, carrots, basil, garlic, oregano, bay leaves, wine vinegar, a little olive oil, and no salt or sugar—you'll start appreciating the more subtle flavors.

Once you begin eating Italian foods prepared more healthfully, your taste buds will become accustomed to the plainer tastes. You will appreciate chicken, lean red meat, fish, and barely cooked vegetables seasoned with spices, herbs, vinegar, or fruit juices—made to order with olive oil instead of butter—and *polenta* instead of the fattier dishes made with *pancetta* (Italian bacon) and *prosciutto* (Italian ham).

Cheese and Dairy Products

Although people often eliminate cheese and other diary products when they want to lose weight, because of milk intolerance, or to maintain a low-cholesterol diet, in actuality these foods provide vitamins and minerals essential to good health.

Milk and dairy products are our richest source of calcium. Don't avoid them unless you have a *lactose intolerance* (the inability to digest sugar in milk or cheese) and taking lactase doesn't help. Don't eliminate any major food group. Dairy products can provide 75 percent of the dietary calcium each of us needs. Adolescents and young adults through age twenty-four require 1,200 milligrams of calcium daily; pregnant women require 1,200 to 1,500 milligrams; and all others, 800. So it's a good idea to regularly include nonfat dairy products in your diet even if you're avoiding cholesterol.

For most men and women, however, cheese should be limited to approximately 2½ ounces per serving, because it's high in fat. When cheeses are used in moderation, you obtain the flavor and some of the calcium you need. Try to select Italian dishes that contain small amounts of nonfat dairy products, or only a little cheese. One tablespoon of *parmigiano-reggiano* grated fresh will flavor any dish.

The following chart shows the descriptions and calorie counts of the more popular Italian cheeses.

Italian Cheese

Cheese	*Description*	*Calories/Oz.*
Asiago	Sheep's milk cheese	110
Di Capra	Goat cheese	76
Emmenthal	Italian Swiss cheese	110
Fontina		120
Gorgonzola		92
Gruyère	Italians call it *groviera*	90
Mascarpone	Cheese from the cream of cow's milk	121
Mozzarella		76
Parmigiano-reggiano	Best *grana*, grated	130
Pecorino	Sheep's milk cheese	120
Provolone	Cow's milk cheese	135
Ricotta	Like cottage cheese, low in salt. Made from condensed milk from sheep and cows	110

The chart below shows you how to supplement your daily requirement of calcium with nondairy high-calcium foods.

Nondairy High-Calcium Foods

Foods	*Milligrams/Calcium*
Vegetables:	
Artichoke, steamed, 1 large	102
Broccoli, steamed, 1 cup	132
Collards, steamed, 1 cup	304
Kale, steamed, 1 cup	249
Turnip greens, steamed, 1 cup	276
Fruits:	
Figs, dried, 5 medium	126
Orange, fresh, 1 large	50
Prunes, dried, 10 uncooked	20
Protein Foods:	
Salmon, pink, canned, ½ cup	245

Nondairy High-Calcium Foods

Foods	*Milligrams/Calcium*
Sardines, canned, 6 medium	266
Tofu (soy bean curd), 2½- by 2¾- by 2-inch piece	300
Miscellaneous:	
Molasses, blackstrap, 1 tbs.	116
Sesame seeds, unhulled, 2 tbs.	210
Tortilla, corn, 6-inch diameter	60

PASTA

If you're like most people, *pasta* is paramount on your list of favorite foods. Italians and Americans alike feel there's something about *pasta*—particularly when it's fresh—that's so good, nothing else can take its place. Nutritionally speaking, at 210 calories for a two-ounce serving and only a trace of fat, it is one of the healthiest foods. But smother it with heavy cream sauces and it becomes a high-fat, high-cholesterol meal. *Pasta* comes in at least six hundred shapes and several colors such as: orange, yellow, red, and green. They're colored with carrot, bell pepper, beet, spinach, and artichoke juices.

Here's a list of the more popular pasta shapes and their descriptions, so you can order the types you enjoy most.

Pasta Shape	*Description*
Agnolotti	Round ravioli filled with meat
Cannelloni	Flat squares of pasta rolled around a stuffing
Capelli d'angeli	"Angel hair," the thinnest pasta
Cappelletti	"Little hats," flat or round squares with filling
Conchiglie	Shell-shaped pasta
Farfalle	Butterfly, ribbon bows
Fettuccine	Flat noodles, ¼-inch wide; delicious fresh

Pasta Shape	*Description*
Fusilli	A spiral, curly spaghetti twisted like a corkscrew
Lasagne	A wide, flat pasta used in baked dishes
Linguini	Flat noodles ⅛-inch wide (my personal favorite)
Manicotti	Hollow pastas; there are more than twenty sizes
Orecchiette	"Little ears," round pasta easily filled with sauce
Penne	Short tubular pasta
Ravioli	Filled pasta squares
Rigatoni	Large, tubular pasta cut into 3-inch lengths
Spaghetti	Dried, thin, long strands of pasta
Tortellini	Small, stuffed twists
Vermicelli	Very thin spaghetti

Pizza—Italian Fast Food

Thank goodness the Italian fast-food situation isn't bleak, because everyone loves *pizza*—the world's favorite pie. In fact, there are more than 38,000 *pizza* restaurants and *pizzerias* in the United States. You can also order healthful and delicious Italian fast foods at *pizza* parlors, juice bars, delis, healthy fast-food takeouts, full-service restaurants, and international chains.

If you're going to eat *pizza* regularly, you may as well turn it into a healthful food. *Peperoni* is the classic meat topping, but when tuna, chicken, or turkey is substituted, an otherwise high-fat food can be turned into a nutritious meal.

The following chart shows the calorie and fat content of two typical *pizza* parlor chains.

Restaurant	*Item*	*Calories*	*Fat*
Domino's	Two slices from a 12-inch cheese pizza	340	16% from fat
Pizza Hut	Two slices from a 13-inch "Thin 'n' Crispy Cheese" pizza	374	26% from fat

To reduce the fat and calories in places like Domino's and Pizza Hut, request half the amount of part-skim milk *mozzarella* cheese and ask for additional fresh tomatoes, mushrooms, and green peppers.

Helene Swerenton, Ph.D., Cooperative Extension nutritionist of the University of California, Davis, puts it this way: "*Pizza* should not be looked at merely as an unhealthful fast food. If properly made, a *pizza* can be very nutritious, containing items from the major food groups. With a flour-based crust, tomato sauce, and *mozzarella* cheese, it offers protein, vitamins, and carbohydrates all in one fairly low-fat package."

I advise inquiring what kind of oil the restaurant uses to make the dough. If it's made with coconut oil, order something else.

Since *pizza* is made to order, here are a few suggestions for turning this delicious item into a healthful fast-food selection.

- Ask for ample amounts of sauce but moderate amounts of cheese.
- Request that vegetable toppings such as onions, eggplant, fresh tomato, zucchini, bell peppers, and mushrooms be freely used.
- Avoid meats such as *peperoni* and salami to lower the fat content and avoid nitrates (a preservative associated with cancer).
- Eat a salad with your fast-food *pizza* meal for nutritional balance and to reduce the number of slices you'll need to feel full. Remember, however, one tablespoon of salad dressing will add seventy to ninety calories.

With one slice of *pizza* and a small salad made with two cups of romaine lettuce, sprouts, carrots, sliced cucumbers, sliced tomato, and very little dressing, you can leave the restaurant feeling satisfied but not stuffed. For variety, have a submarine or meatball sandwich with a salad. On the sub, simply substitute turkey for salami, hold the mayo, and use mustard instead. Before ordering a meatball sandwich, make sure it's made with lean beef instead of sausage.

TRATTORIAS

You won't need to make many modifications at *La Scala* in Brentwood, California, since there, traditional Italian cooking has been influenced by the new "California cuisine." They serve health-food *pizzas* made with fresh produce and seasonal ingredients, they grill their meats, and their *pasta* is made without oil.

Today, almost every cosmopolitan neighborhood has a *trattoria* (quiet, informal Italian restaurant). When you want to dine, formal *ristoranti* are enjoyable, but *trattorias* are more fun. **The checkmarks indicate the dishes I recommend.**

▲

LA SCALA PRESTO TRATTORIA MENU

Antipasti

Mozzarella Marinara
  Breaded Cheese and Tomato Sauce
√ Panzanella
  Tuscan Salad of Tomatoes, Cucumbers, Bell Peppers, Peasant Bread with Balsamic Vinegar
Pepperoni Abbracciati con Alici
  Roasted Peppers with Anchovies
Prosciutto & Melone
  Italian Ham with Melon
Carpaccio
  Thinly Sliced Raw Beef
Mozzarella Buffala a la Caprese
  With Tomatoes, Basil and Virgin Olive Oil
√ Insalata di Calamari
  Squid Salad

√ = Recommended

√ Bruschetta
Peasant Bread with Garlic & Tomato

Insalate

√ Leon Chopped Salad [Substitute turkey]
√ Insalata Mista Verde
Mixed Green Salad
√ Caesar Salad [If the dressing contains raw egg, request herb]

Zuppa

√ Minestrone
√ Zuppa All' Ortolana
Puree of Vegetables

Pollo

√ Pollo al Forno
Baked Chicken
√ Pollo Cacciatore
Tomato, Mushrooms, Bell Peppers

Dolci

Cheese Cake
Crostata di Frutta
Fruit Tart
Chocolate Mousse
Gelato di Casa
Homemade Ice Cream

Pizze

√ Pizza Margherita
Cheese, Tomato, Basil
√ Pizza Ai Funghi
Fresh Mushrooms, Mozzarella
√ Pizza Vegetariana
√ Pizza al Buon Gusto
To Your Liking
√ Pizza Presto "Arrabiata"
Virgin Olive Oil, Onion, Chili Pepper, Cheese
Calzone al Forno
Stuffed with Mozzarella, Ricotta, Spinach, Mushrooms, Parmigiana

√ = Recommended

Pasta

√ Spaghetti Pomodoro & Basilico
With Tomato and Basil

√ Tagliatelle Verde
With Mushrooms and Marinara Sauce

Spaghetti Carbonara con Funghi
With Bacon, Cream, Mushrooms

√ Linguini al Pesto
Basil, Olive Oil, Garlic, Pine Nuts

Lasagne Verde

Spaghetti con Salsiccie
Italian Sausage and Peppers

√ Ravioli Tre Colore
Chicken, Ricotta

Melanzana al Forno
Baked Eggplant with Tomato and Mozzarella

√ Capelli D'Angeli Primavera
With Vegetables

√ Spaghetti Alla Checca
Fresh Tomatoes, Olive Oil, Garlic, Basil

Bucatini All' Amatriciana
Bacon, Peppers, Tomato Sauce

Bevande

√ Espresso
Coffee
Tea
√ Cappuccino
√ Mineral Water
Coca-Cola
Tab
Sprite
Beer
Imported Beer

House Wine Glass / Half Carafe / Full Bottle

▼

√ = **Recommended**

✓TO CHOOSE

If you're one of *chi non vuole ingrassare* (those people who do not want to put on weight), this Italian Menu Command will make ordering healthfully in Italian restaurants easier for you. These dishes, all lower in fat, salt, sugar, and calories, can be found on most Italian menus.

Drinks (Bevande)

Caffè (coffee): Drink regular coffee in moderation, health permitting before 4:00 P.M. so it doesn't interfere with your sleep.
Caffè latte (coffee with milk): request nonfat milk.
Cappuccino (coffee with steamed milk): request nonfat milk and decaffeinated coffee if it's late in the day.
Espresso (request decaffeinated if it's late in the day)
Ferrarelle (mineral water)
Fonte Viva (mineral water): my personal favorite
Sanka (instant decaffeinated coffee)
S. Pellegrino (mineral water)
Succo di pomodoro (tomato juice): if you can have salt
Te (tea): caffeinated or herbal
Una spremuta d' arancia/di limone/di pompelmo (fresh-squeezed orange, lemon, grapefruit juice)

***Choose* beverages whenever possible that don't contain alcohol, caffeine, or sugar.**
***BEST BETS:* Fonte Viva, fresh juice, or decaffeinated *cappuccino* topped with nonfat whipped milk, a sprinkle of cinnamon, and a dusting of chocolate.**

Appetizers (Antipasti)

Antipasti di molluschi (assorted shellfish)
Asparagi (asparagus)

✓ TO CHOOSE

Bresaola (air-dried cured beef usually topped with artichoke hearts and lemon)

Bruschetta al pomodoro (grilled Italian bread topped with tomatoes or arugula): request yours without both butter and olive oil or with olive oil only

Calamaretti (baby octopus or squids)

Cape Sante al radicchio (scallops wrapped in radicchio)

Caponata (eggplant appetizer)

Carciofi (artichokes)

Carciofi al forno (artichokes baked in a covered pan with olive oil, garlic, and parsley)

Carpaccio (paper-thin slices of raw beef usually topped with capers, arugula, and shavings of cheese, served cold): capers contain salt

Cozze della riviera (mussels steamed in red sauce)

Funghi marinati (marinated mushrooms)

Melanzane alla romana (baked eggplant with sauce, basil, and cheese

Melone (melon)

Ostriche (oysters): if they're cooked

Peperonata (sliced red pimentos, tomatoes, and onions sautéed in olive oil)

Peperoncini arrostiti (roasted peppers)

Pizzetta con aglio (small *pizza* with garlic): eat garlic often, it may lower your cancer risk

Pomodori ripieni (tomato stuffed with meat, bread crumbs, rice, or *macaroni*)

Pompelmo (grapefruit)

Radici or *rapanelli* (radishes)

Sarde all' olio (sardines in oil): make sure they're in olive oil or another healthful one

Scampi saltati (sautéed shrimps): make sure they're cooked in olive oil

✓To Choose

Sott' aceti (mixed vegetables in plain vinegar)
Vongole e cozze al vino bianco (clams and mussels steamed in white wine)

***Choose* dishes with marinara, red clam, or mussel sauce.**
***BEST BETS: Caponata* (eggplant appetizer), *antipasti di molluschi* (assorted shellfish), or *Pizzetta con aglio* (small pizza with garlic).**

Soup (Zuppa)

Brodo (broth or consommé)
Brodo di pollo (chicken broth)
Cassola (fish stew)
Celestina (clear soup with little stars of *pasta*)
Minestra (fresh vegetable soup)
Minestrone (fresh vegetables cooked with beans and either *pasta* or rice)
Pasta e fagioli (soup with beans and *pasta*)
Pastina in brodo (consommé with *pastina*): request *pasta* without egg yolk
Ribollita (beans, black cabbage, other vegetables, and bread at the bottom to thicken the soup)
Stracciatella (chicken soup)
Stracciatella fiorentina (Italian chicken soup): a free-form dumpling filled with spinach in a delicate broth
Zuppa alla marinara (fish stew)
Zuppa di cozze (mussel soup)
Zuppa di fagioli con la pasta (bean soup with *pasta*)
Zuppa di fagioli ed orzo (bean and barley soup)
Zuppa di pesce (simple fish broth; often called *brodetto*)
Zuppa di spinaci (spinach soup)
Zuppa di vongole (clams steamed in white wine and shallots)

✓TO CHOOSE

Choose **stewlike soups containing rice, beans, *pasta*, and lentils.**

BEST BETS: Minestrone **(fresh-cooked vegetables with beans and either *pasta* or rice), or *zuppa di pesce* (simple fish broth).**

Breads (Pane)

Baghetta (sourdough Italian bread)
Bruschetta (peasant bread with garlic and tomato: order with olive oil instead of butter
Ciabatta (flat bread): shaped like a slipper
Focaccia (bread that's eaten as a snack in Italy)
Michetta (hollow roll with a circle at the top and wedges on the side)
Pane Integrale (whole wheat bread)

Choose **breads made with soy, safflower, olive, or canola oil.**

BEST BET: Bruschetta

Pizza (Pizza)

Calzone (a folded pizza): request healthful fillings and only a little cheese
Pizza (dough covered with a variety of toppings): make sure it doesn't contain coconut oil
Pizza alla mozzarella (tomato and *mozzarella* cheese)
Pizza al pomodoro (tomato, no cheese)
Pizza al rosmarino (with rosemary)
Pizza vegetale (vegetarian *pizza*)

Choose pizza **if the dough is made with soy, safflower, olive, canola, or any of the other good oils. Go light with the cheese, and heavy with the toppings.**

✓To Choose

BEST BET: Pizza vegetale **(vegetarian *pizza*)**

Pasta (Pastasciutta)

Capelli d'angeli (angel's hair pasta): order it with marinara sauce

Fettuccine col sugo di vongole e zucchine (*fettuccine* with clams and zucchini)

Gnocchi all' onda (pieces of *pasta* dough filled with potatoes and decorated with a fork): order them when made without eggs

Gnocchi verdi (green dumplings)

Lasagne (flat noodles layered with cheese, tomato sauce, and sometimes chicken or beef)

Lasagne al pesto (*lasagne* with *pesto* sauce)

Lasagne con le verdure (vegetable *lasagne*; wide strips of *pasta* layered in a casserole)

Linguine alle vongole (*linguine* in clam sauce): choose the red and the white if it is not made with milk or cream

Manicotti (large round *pasta* noodles stuffed with *ricotta*, *mozzarella*, and *parmigiano* cheeses, parsley, and nutmeg)

Pasta ai funghi (mushroom *pasta*)

Pasta primavera (*pasta* mixed with vegetables): avoid cream sauces

Pasta rossa (red beet *pasta*)

Pasta verde (spinach *pasta*)

Penne alla checca (*pasta* topped with chopped raw tomatoes)

Ravioli di melanzane (eggplant *ravioli*)

Ravioli di ricotta (*ricotta* cheese *ravioli*)

Scampi in busera (*spaghetti* with shrimp)

Spaghetti al filetto (*spaghetti* in a fresh tomato sauce)

Spaghetti al funghi freschi (*spaghetti* with fresh mushrooms)

✓ To Choose

Spaghetti al sugo (*spaghetti* with meat sauce)
Spaghetti con asparagi e pomodoro (*spaghetti* with asparagus and tomato)
Spaghetti coi polipi (*spaghetti* with baby octopus)
Spaghettini con le cozze (thin *spaghetti* with mussels)
Tagliatelle alla romagnola con sugo di spinaci (noodles with spinach and tomato)

Choose **marinara sauce seasoned with fresh tomatoes, carrots, basil, garlic, oregano, bay leaves, Italian parsley, and wine vinegar.**

BEST BETS: Pasta primavera (pasta **mixed with vegetables) or *penne alla checca* (*pasta* topped with chopped fresh tomatoes)**

Rice (Riso), Cornmeal Mixture (Polenta), and Bean (Fagioli) Dishes

Fagioli (white beans): cooked in many ways
Fagioli toscanelli con tonno (white bean and tuna salad)
Pasta e ceci (*macaroni* and chickpeas)
Pasta e fagioli (*macaroni* and beans)
Polenta (a cornmeal, water, and flour mixture): can be ordered freshly made or cooled and grilled
Riso (rice)
Riso alla saracena (rice with finely chopped shellfish)
Riso e zucca (rice and pumpkin)
Riso in bianco (boiled white rice)
Riso verde (rice with sage and chopped spinach)
Risotto bianco (*risotto* cooked with water, broth, and white wine instead of butter)
Risotto con carciofi (*risotto* with baby artichokes)
Risotto con pesce (*risotto* with fish): *risotto* with fish or shellfish is usually cooked with olive oil instead of butter

✓TO CHOOSE

Risotto di frutti di mare (*risotto* with shellfish)
Risotto di vongole (*risotto* with clams)
Risotto mari e monti (*risotto* with tiny shrimp and mushrooms): delicious and very satisfying

Choose **rice, cornmeal, and bean dishes made without butter. Beans are an important part of any meal—especially vegetarian—because they're high in fiber and protein.**
BEST BETS: Polenta **(a cornmeal, water, and flour mixture),** ***riso alla saracena*** **(rice with finely chopped shellfish),** ***risotto mari e monti*** **(*****risotto*** **with tiny shrimp and mushrooms).**

Sauces (Salsas)

Aglio e olio (garlic, olive oil, and parsley): request less oil
Cacciatora (juniper-flavored meat and vegetable sauce)
Filetto (fresh tomato sauce)
Frutti di mare (seafood sauce)
Gamberetti (sauce with large shrimps)
Marinara (a sauce of fresh tomatoes, parsley, olive oil, and basil accented with garlic): request without oil
Napoletana (tomato sauce flavored with herbs)
Peperoni (sweet peppers, tomato, garlic sauce)
Pesto alla genovese (*pesto* sauce): fresh basil, garlic, pine nuts, imported *parmigiano* cheese, and olive oil; ask the chef to go light on the sauce
Pizzaiola (hot tomato sauce with hot peppers and herbs)
Pomodoro (plum tomato sauce with onions, celery, garlic, fresh basil, and spices)
Ricotta (*ricotta* cheese mixed with *pasta*)
Romana (meat and chicken sauce with mushrooms)

✓TO CHOOSE

Salsa di pomodoro piccante (spicy tomato sauce): be sure it's not too oily
Sarde (sauce containing sardines, spices, and olive oil)
Sugo di mare (seafood sauce)
Sugo di pomodoro (tomato sauce): request without oil
Veneziana (tomato sauce): request without oil
Vongole (clam sauce with onions, tomatoes, olive oil, and garlic): request the red sauce, not the white

***Choose* red sauces made without butter or a lot of oil.**
***BEST BETS: Frutti di mare* (seafood sauce), *pomodoro* (plum tomatoes with onions, celery, garlic, fresh basil and spices)**

Egg Dishes (Uova)

Affogate con punte di asparagi (eggs poached with asparagus tips)
Affogate in pomodoro (eggs poached in tomato sauce)
Frittata con basilico (omelet seasoned with basil)
Frittata con carciofi (omelet with artichoke hearts)
Frittata con maccheroni (omelet with cooked *pasta*)
Frittata di cipolle (onion omelet)
Frittata di funghi (mushroom omelet)
Frittata di patate (potato omelet)
Frittata genovese (spinach omelet)
Uova affogate (poached eggs)
Uova mollette (soft-boiled eggs)
Uova sode (hard-boiled eggs)
Uova stracciate (scrambled eggs)

***Choose* egg dishes occasionally if your cholesterol level is not too high. Ask the chef to throw away one or more of the yolks and to use oil instead of butter.**

✓TO CHOOSE

***BEST BETS: Frittata di funghi* (mushroom omelet), *uova affogate* (poached eggs).**

Fish (Pesci)

Aragosta fra' diavolo (lobster braised with wine and tomatoes)
Branzino alla griglia (grilled red snapper)
Brodetto (fish stew with oil, tomato, garlic, onion, and wine vinegar)
Calamari barcaiola (squid in white wine sauce with shallots and tomato)
Calamari ripieni di peperoni rossi (squid stuffed with red peppers)
Cappe saltate al rosmarino e limone (sautéed scallops with rosemary and lemon)
Cassola (fish stew)
Coregono (lake whitefish): my personal favorite
Cozze á vapore (steamed mussels)
Crostacei (shellfish)
Gamberetti (little prawns)
Gamberi (big prawns)
Ostriche (oysters): make sure they're cooked
Pesce passera (flounder)
Pesce persico (perch)
Pesce spada al forno (baked swordfish)
Pesce spada alla griglia (grilled swordfish steaks)
Salmone (salmon)
Sampietro (John Dory)
Sarde (sardines)
Sardelline (young sardines)
Scampi al vino bianco (shrimps sautéed in white wine): request olive oil
Scampi fra' diavolo (shrimps sautéed in a tomato sauce)

✓ To Choose

Sogliola (sole)
Spigola bollita (poached striped bass)
Trota (trout)
Trota salmonata (salmon trout)
Vongole veneziana (clams steamed in white wine)

***Choose* fish dishes often. Their omega-3 fatty acids help protect against heart disease.**
***BEST BETS: Aragosta fra' diavolo* (lobster braised with wine and tomatoes), *coregono* (lake whitefish), or *vongole o cozze veneziana* (clams or mussels steamed in white wine)**

Chicken (Pollo)

Costoletta di pollo (breast of chicken)
Petti di pollo (breast of chicken)
Pollo al forno (chicken baked in the oven)
Pollo al peperoni (chicken cooked with pimentos, tomatoes, white wine, and herbs)
Pollo al vino bianco (pieces of chicken cooked slowly in white wine)
Pollo alla cacciatora (chicken cacciatore—chicken cooked in garlic, onion, mushrooms, tomatoes, and herbs)
Pollo alle erbe (chicken with herbs)
Pollo alla griglia (grilled chicken)
Pollo alla griglia al limone (broiled lemon chicken)
Pollo alla padovana (chicken highly spiced and roasted)
Pollo alla zingara (chicken baked in a clay pot)
Pollo arrostito (roasted chicken)
Pollo bianco (chicken with onion, celery, herbs, parsley, and basil)
Pollo francese (boneless breast of chicken in white wine)

✓TO CHOOSE

Pollo grillettato all' arentina (chicken cooked with onions, peas, rice, and white wine)
Pollo in piccata (chicken sautéed in olive oil and lemon juice)
Pollo in umido (chicken cooked with vegetables in a covered pan)
Pollo lesso (boiled chicken)
Pollo napoletana (chicken cooked slowly with mushrooms, tomatoes, onions, garlic, and wine)
Pollo potenzese (chicken roasted with potatoes, garlic, and grated cheese)
Pollo primavera (chicken with vegetables)

***Choose* skinless chicken dishes made without butter. (White meat chicken has less calories than dark meat.)**
***BEST BETS: Pollo in piccata* (chicken sautéed in olive oil and lemon juice), *pollo alla cacciatora* (chicken cacciatore), *pollo alla griglia al limone* (broiled lemon chicken), or *pollo alla zingara* (chicken baked in a clay pot).**

Turkey (Tacchino)

Filetti di tacchino (breast of turkey slices)
Rotolo di tacchino (turkey meat boned and rolled)
Stufato al vino bianco (stewed turkey with white wine, herbs, vegetables, and mushrooms)
Tacchino Arrosto (turkey roasted)
Tacchino Bollito (turkey boiled with vegetables)

***Choose* white meat turkey dishes made without butter.**
Turkey is high in protein and low in fat. Eat it often.
BEST BET: Tacchino arrosto

✓ To Choose

Beef (Carni)

Bistecca (beefsteak): make sure it's lean
Bistecca alla cacciatora (beef with wine and tomato sauce flavored with garlic and parsley)
Bistecca alla pizzaiola (tomato sauce spread over lean beef)
Bistecca con funghi porcini (grilled steak with *porcini* mushrooms)
Bistecca di manzo (sirloin steak): 3½ ounces equals one serving
Bistecchini ascé alla griglia (hamburger): make sure it's lean.
Brasato con lenticchie (braised beef with lentils)
Bresaola (cured beef)
Costa di bue al brasato (sirloin of beef braised with vegetables)
Garofolato (beef flavored with cloves, red wine, and vegetables)
Medaglioni di bue (mignonettes of beef)

***Choose* lean cuts of beef. Depending upon how it is prepared, meat can be a healthy entrée or a fatty one. Request yours baked or roasted in the oven (*al forno*), braised (*brasato*), grilled (*alla griglia*), or on the spit (*allo spiedo*) the way you like it—rare (*al sangue*), medium (*cotta a puntino*), or well done (*ben cotta*).**
***BEST BET: Bistecca di manzo* (sirloin steak)**

Salads (Insalata) and Vegetables (Legumi)

Broccoletti (broccoli)
Carciofi alla romana (steamed artichoke)
Carote (carrots)

✓To Choose

Cavolfiore (cauliflower)
Cavoli di brusselle (Brussels sprouts)
Cavolo (cabbage)
Ceci (chickpeas)
Cetrioli (cucumbers)
Cima di rape (turnip tops)
Cipolle (onions)
Crescione (watercress)
Fagiolini marinara (string beans sautéed in marinara sauce)
Fave (broad beans): sometimes eaten raw as an *antipasto*
Finocchio (fennel)
Funghi (mushrooms)
Funghi trifolati (sautéed mushrooms): make sure they're in olive oil
Il fricandó (an assortment of cooked vegetables)
Insalata cesare (Caesar salad): request an alternate dressing
Insalata composta (mixed salad)
Insalata cotta (cooked vegetable salad)
Insalata di fagiolini (green bean salad)
Insalata di gamberi (shrimp salad)
Insalata di limone, cetriolo, e peperone (lemon, cucumber, and pepper salad)
Insalata di pomodoro (tomato salad)
Insalata mista (mixed salad): order without olives and cheese; use wine vinegar or lemon juice as a dressing with a touch of olive oil
Lattuga e pomodoro (lettuce and tomato): use wine vinegar or lemon juice as a dressing with a touch of olive oil
Melanzane parmigiana (eggplant *parmigiana*): ask that only a small amount of skim-milk *mozzarella* is used
Panzanella (tomatoes, cored cucumbers, bell pepper slices, and chunks of Italian bread tossed with vinaigrette)

✓To Choose

Patate in veste da camera (baked potato)
Patate lesse (boiled potato): *non condite* (plain)
Patatine (sweet potatoes)
Pomodori ripieni (stuffed tomatoes)
Radicchio (a type of lettuce with a slightly bitter taste): has a delicious, smoky taste when grilled and tossed with a light vinaigrette dressing
Rape (turnips)
Rucola (arugula)
Spinaci (spinach)
Verdure alla griglia (grilled vegetables): ask the chef to go light on the olive oil
Zucchini bolliti (zucchini steamed)

Choose **dark green lettuce salads dressed with crushed garlic, basil, or other fresh herbs, lemon juice, balsamic or wine vinegar, and very little oil.**
BEST BETS: Radicchio **or** ***insalata cesare*** **with a light olive oil–base dressing**

Desserts (Dolci e Gelati)

Cappuccino
Fragole all' aceto balsamico (macerated strawberries with balsamic vinegar)
Fragole fresche (fresh strawberries)
Frutta ai ferri (grilled fruit)
Frutta cotta (stewed fruit)
Frutta di stagione (fruit of the season)
Frutta fresca (fresh fruit)
Granita (Italian ice)
Lamponi (raspberries)
Macedonia di frutta (fresh fruit salad)

✓ TO CHOOSE

Macedonia di stagione o secca (fruit salad in season)
Mela (apple)
Melone di stagione (melon in season)
Pan de Spagna (sponge cake)
Pere al forno (baked pears)
Pere cotte con alloro e amarone (braised pears with bay leaves and red wine)
Polenta (cornmeal porridge): sometimes made with milk and sweetened for dessert
Sorbetto di albicocca (apricot sorbet)
Sorbetto di cocomero e limone (watermelon and lemon sorbet)
Sorbetto di mela dorata (golden apple sorbet)
Sorbetto di melagrana (pomegranate sorbet)

***Choose* desserts that are low in fat and don't contain a lot of sugar.**
***BEST BETS: Fragole fresche* (fresh strawberries), *melone di stagione* (melon in season), or *sorbetti* (sorbet)**

⊘ TO AVOID

Drinks

Alpini, Amaretto, Anisetta, Fiori, Grappa, and Strega: after-dinner cocktails that contain a lot of sugar
Espresso (Italian black coffee): contains too much caffeine
Vino (wine): not recommended, although the Italians make some of the best—Valpolicella (a dark mellow red), Chianti (a pleasing red wine), Ravello rosato (a delicate rosé), Soave (a white delicate wine), and Orvieto (a fruity white wine)

⊘TO AVOID

Avoid **drinking alcoholic beverages, especially those containing a lot of sugar.**

Appetizers

Affettati misti (sliced ham, sausages, and other cold meats)
Antipasto (hors d'oeuvres): avoid the olives, ham, sausages, and salty fish
Bondiola di Parma (pork sausage from northern Italy)
Calamari fritti (deep-fried squid)
Carciofi alla maionese (artichoke hearts with mayonnaise)
Carciofi dorati (artichokes dipped in egg and flour and fried)
Chizze (squares of pastry filled with anchovy and cheese)
Coppa (salami): made from pig's head, neck muscles, and rind
Crostini (pieces of bread covered with cheese, chicken livers, or pâté)
Fonduta (hot melted cheese with toast)
Lingua (tongue)
Lumache (snails)
Melanzane alla Romagna (eggplant sliced, dipped in egg, and fried)
Mozzarella marinara (fried *mozzarella* sandwich with tomato sauce)
Olive al forno (black olives in a sauce of white wine, rosemary, and garlic)
Pate di fegato (liver pâté)
Pate di fegato di pollo (chicken liver pâté)
Prosciutto (ham): too fatty
Prosciutto affumicato (smoked ham)
Prosciutto con melone (ham with melon)
Prosciutto cotto (cooked ham)
Prosciutto crudo (raw ham)

⊘ TO AVOID

Prosciutto di langhirano (ham from northern Italy)
Rane dorate (frogs' legs dipped in egg and fried)
Salame fabriano (salami made from pork and veal)
Salame di felino (pork salami): very fatty and expensive
Salame genovese (pork, veal, and pork fat salami)
Suppli al telefono (deep-fried rice-and-cheese balls)

***Avoid* dishes containing a lot of cheese or fatty meats.**

Soups

Brodetto pasquale (broth with meat and vegetables thickened with egg yolks)
Busecchina (soup made of chestnuts, wine, and milk)
Crema (cream soup): usually chicken or vegetable; fortunately, Italians rarely add cream to their soups
Minestra con broccoli (broccoli soup): contains butter
Panata (a bread soup with grated cheese and egg)
Pesce alla paesana (fish peasant style): contains butter
Risi e bisi (rice and pea soup flavored with ham)
Zuppa pavese (soup topped with grated cheese and a poached egg): contains butter

***Avoid* soups made with pork rind, egg yolk, butter, or cream.**

Breads

***Avoid* all breads made with the unhealthful hydrogenated oils: coconut or palm.**

Pizza

***Avoid pizza* and *calzone* (*pizza* pocket) dough made with**

⊘ TO AVOID

the unhealthful oils. Also *pizza* topped with cured meats or sausages are too fatty for a healthful diet.

Pasta Dishes

Cannelloni (*pasta* tubes filled with meat and cream sauce and topped with cheese)
Croquette di patate (deep-fried potato balls)
Garganelli (*pasta* with smoked salmon)
Lasagne (large, flat-layered noodles with filling): contains three or more types of cheese and sausage
Linguine with creamy shrimp sauce
Manicotti di ricotta (cheese-filled *pasta* tubes)
Meat *tortellini* (small ovals of *pasta* filled with a filling of lean beef, lean pork, imported *parmigiano* cheese, *prosciutto*, herbs, and spices)
Pasta Alfredo (*fettucinni* with cream, butter, and cheese sauce): choose red sauces rather than white creamy ones
Pasta all' uovo (egg *pasta*): higher in cholesterol than plain *pasta* because it contains egg yolk
Pasta al mascarpone (a rich creamy *pasta* dish): the cheese in this dish alone contains 121 calories per ounce
Pasta di spinaci ai quattro formaggi (spinach *pasta* with four cheeses)
Roselline di pasta alla romagnola (*pasta* roses with ham and *fontina* cheese)
Ruote di carro col sugo di salsicce, panna, e pomodoro (cartwheel-shaped *pasta* with sausages, cream, and tomato)
Spaghetti alla carbonara (with bacon, butter, and raw egg)
Spaghetti all' amatriciana (made with bacon and *pecorino* cheese): fatty

⊘TO AVOID

Spaghettini con pane, acciughe, e olive (thin *spaghetti* with bread crumbs, anchovies, and black olives): too salty

Tortellini gratinati (meat dumplings *au gratin*)

Tortelloni (oversize *tortellini* filled with chicken, *prosciutto*, imported *parmigiano* cheese, herbs, and spices)

***Avoid pastas* stuffed with whole-milk cheeses or fatty meats or topped with creamy sauces.**

Sauces

Acciughe (sauce of anchovies flavored with garlic, oil, and parsley): too oily and salty

Agrodolce (sweet-and-sour sauce)

Alfredo (cream, butter, and *parmigiano* cheese traditionally served with *fettuccine* noodles): choose red sauces over white, creamy ones

Amatriciana (fresh tomatoes, bacon, onion, and garlic): too fatty

Anitra (with duck sauce)

Bagna cauda (garlic and anchovy sauce): contains butter and cream

Balsamella or *Besciamella* (*béchamel* sauce): contains butter and cream

Bianca (white sauce): flavored with cheese

Bolognese (a rich meat sauce flavored with chicken livers and fresh vegetables, sautéed with butter, cream, and red wine, then simmered with veal stock, mushrooms, and plum tomatoes): also called *ragù*; delicious, but fatty.

Burro (butter and grated *parmigiano* cheese)

Carbonara (chopped bacon, scrambled eggs, and grated cheese)

Casalinga (homemade tomato sauce flavored with bacon)

⊘ To Avoid

Ciociara (a sauce containing bacon fat, ham, and sausage)
Doppio formaggio (a sauce with more cheese than usual)
Forestiera (tomato sauce, sliced zucchini, mushrooms, and onions sautéed with *prosciutto, parmigiano* cheese, and heavy cream)
Forno (baked *pasta* with cheese and butter sauce)
Funghi e piselli (bacon, mushrooms, and fresh green peas)
Genovese (chopped veal, vegetables, mushrooms, tomatoes, and white wine)
Graneresi (a sauce of pounded walnuts, cream cheese, and garlic)
Maionese (mayonnaise): hold the mayo!
Mantovana (a sauce of pounded walnuts, white wine, cream, and butter)
Noci (chopped pine nuts and walnuts, oil, garlic, and parsley): nuts are very fatty
Olandese (Hollandaise)
Paesana (a sauce of mushrooms, bacon fat, tomatoes, herbs, and cheese)
Panna (a sauce containing hot cream)
Quattro formaggi (a sauce containing four cheeses: *fontina, Gruyère, parmigiano*, and *provolone dolce*)
Ragù (sometimes called *bolognese*): contains butter and cream
Spuma (a sauce of hot cream and chopped ham)
Tartufata (truffles, butter, white wine, and garlic)
Trasteverina (tomato sauce with white wine, chopped bacon, and chicken livers)
Triestina (a meat sauce with chopped ham, butter, and cream)
Umbria (anchovy paste, oil, garlic, tomatoes, and truffles)
Villeroy (white sauce): thickened with egg yolk and flavored with ham and cheese

⊘ TO AVOID

Villeroy (white sauce): thickened with egg yolk and flavored with ham and cheese

***Avoid* creamy, buttery cheesy sauces.**

Rice, Polenta, Bean Dishes

Arancini (deep-fried, cheese-filled rice balls)
Insalata saporita (rice salad): usually contains sausage
Risotto (Italian medium-grain white rice): contains too much butter and sometimes cheese
Risotto alla milanese (risotto milanese): a stickier style of *risotto* made with butter, grated *parmigiano* cheese, and saffron
Risotto all' onda (wavy or slightly runny consistency): made with too much butter

***Avoid* rice, *polenta*, and bean dishes when they are made with a lot of butter.**

Egg Dishes

Cacciatora (eggs poached in tomato sauce with chicken livers)
Frittata al formaggio (cheese omelet)
Fritte al bacon (fried eggs and bacon)
Uova affrittellate (fried eggs cooked in butter)
Uova al burro (eggs cooked in butter in the oven)
Uova alla piemontese (eggs cooked with *Gruyère* cheese)
Uova con panna (hard-boiled eggs with cream sauce)
Uova con parmigiana (eggs baked with ham and grated cheese)
Uova con piselli (eggs with bacon and peas on top)

⊘ TO AVOID

Uova con prosciutto e mozzarella (baked eggs on top of ham and cheese)
Uova sode con salsa maionese (hard-boiled eggs with mayonnaise)
Uova strapazzate con la salsiccia (scrambled eggs with sausage)

***Avoid* egg dishes that contain butter, bacon, ham, or a lot of cheese.**

Fish

Acciughe (anchovies): too salty
Anguilla marinata (deep-fried eel)
Aringhe (herring): usually contains cream
Bigné di pesci misti (deep-fried seafood)
Branzino in burro e prezzemolo (sea bass or turbot with butter and parsley)
Filetti di sogliola alla fiorentina (fillet of sole Florentine style)
Gamberi gratinati allo zabaione (steamed shrimp with *zabaglione* sauce): usually contains egg yolk
Molecche (soft-shell crabs): usually cooked in butter
Scampi (shrimp cooked in butter)
Trota in padella (pan-fried trout): usually breaded and cooked in butter

***Avoid* seafood that is deep-fried or cooked in butter.**

Chicken

Arrosto alla bolognese (chicken roasted in butter and oil with ham and garlic)

⊘ To Avoid

Castellana (two pieces of chicken with ham and cheese between)

Crocchette di pollo dorate (chicken dipped in egg and bread crumbs and then fried)

Dorato (chicken coated with flour and egg and then deep-fried)

Filetti di pollo alla modenese (chicken cooked with ham and cheese)

Fiorentina (chicken fried in butter)

Gambe di pollo farcite (chicken drumsticks stuffed with ham and cheese)

Mantovana (chicken sautéed in butter and garnished with olives)

Marsala (chicken fried in butter, and served with Marsala wine)

Milanese (chicken dipped in an egg and bread crumb mixture and then fried)

Olive (chicken sautéed with vegetables and olives): olives are high in calories

Pollo alla cavour (chicken cooked in butter with slices of ham and cheese and served with a truffle sauce)

Pollo alla panna (chicken cooked in cream and butter)

Pollo arrosto con la pancetta e gli odori (roast chicken with *pancetta* and herbs): contains Italian bacon

Pollo con le cipolle (fricasseed chicken with onions): contains a lot of oil

Pollo con salsiccia (chicken with sausage)

Porchetta (chicken stuffed with ham, garlic, and fennel)

Romana (pieces of chicken cooked in a pan with onion, ham, pimentos, oil, and butter

Sovrana (chicken with artichokes and a cream sauce)

Tetrazzini (chicken in a casserole with layers of *pasta* and a rich sauce)

⊘ TO AVOID

Valdostana (chicken cooked with cheese, white truffles, white wine, and brandy)

***Avoid* fried chicken and chicken cooked with bacon, sausage, or ham.**

Turkey

Arrosto tartufato (roasted with Marsala, truffles, and butter)
Bolognese (cooked with ham and cheese)
Burro (cooked in butter)
Gallinaccio brodettato (turkey with a thick cream sauce thickened with egg yolk)
Margaret Rose (turkey cooked with ham and cheese in a pastry shell)
Marsala (cooked in butter and Marsala)
Modenese (with slices of ham and cheese)
Pasticcio (in *pasta* with a cream sauce)
Prosciutto (turkey with ham)
Tetrazzini (turkey with *pasta* in a creamy mushroom sauce)

***Avoid* turkey with cream, butter, or cheese sauce.**

Beef

Asticciole alla calabrese (rolled beef with cheese, sausage, and squares of bread, dipped in oil and grilled)
Braciolettine ripiene (stuffed beef and ham rolls cooked in butter and wine)
Rolè (beef roll filled with ham and hard-boiled eggs and cooked in butter)

⊘ TO AVOID

Pork

Capicolla (ham)
Genoa (salami): often made with pork
Polpettone (meat loaf): often made with sausage
Portafoglio di maiale con fegato di vitello (pork chops stuffed with calf's liver)
Salsicce alla napoletana (spicy Italian sausage)
Salsicce con verdure (sausage with Swiss chard or other vegetables)

***Avoid* fatty cuts of pork and those stuffed with cheese or butter.**

Veal

Bracioline di vitello con l'agnello (veal dish with lamb)
Brocciola (veal roll)
Cotolette alla milanese (breaded veal cutlets)
Nodini di vitello con funghi (sautéed veal chops): too fatty
Ossobuco alla milanese (braised veal shanks): bone with a hole
Polpette (meatballs): contains veal and pork; too fatty
Saltimbocca (veal roll): contains butter and cream
Scaloppine di vitello (veal *scaloppine*): contains butter

***Avoid* the fattier cuts of veal.**

Lamb, Duck, Tongue, and Liver

***Avoid* these meats, they are too fatty for a healthful diet.**

Salads and Vegetables

⊘ To Avoid

Carciofi alla giudia (fried artichokes)
Carciofi con burro e il parmigiano (artichokes with butter and *parmigiano*)
Cipolline in tegame con la pancetta (pearl onions with *pancetta*, rosemary, and vinegar): contains Italian bacon and butter
Divorziate (mashed potato with hard-boiled egg yolks): contains too much cholesterol
Insalata di patate con la pancetta affumicata (potato salad with bacon)
Patate alla padella (fried potatoes)
Tortellini salad with pesto
Zucchine saltate con basilico (sautéed zucchini with basil): contains butter

***Avoid* vegetables made with butter, bacon, or cheese.**

Desserts

Budino (pudding)
Cannoli (a rolled wafer cookie filled with cream or sweetened *ricotta* cheese)
Cassata alla siciliana (Sicilian cake with chocolate frosting)
Crema (custard)
Crema caramella (caramel custard)
Creme brulée (puddinglike dessert): contains sugar and cream
Dolce di riso al forno (baked rice pudding): contains butter, sugar, and milk
Gelati (ice creams)
Gelato all' espresso (*espresso* ice cream)
Gelato caramellato (caramel ice cream)

⊘ TO AVOID

Mascarpone (cheese): all cheeses are high in fat, but this one is outrageous!
Napoleon (flaky pastry layered with fresh peaches and topped with chocolate sauce)
Panettone (coffee cake)
Panforte (cake containing nuts, cocoa, spices, orange peel, and honey)
Spumoni (Italian ice cream)
Tartufi (chocolate truffles)
Tirami su (a creamy pudding, meaning "pick me up" in Italian, with coffee-flavored lady fingers): made with an excess of whipped cream
Torta di amaretti e cioccolato (a cake made of *amaretti* and chocolate)
Torta di frutta alla panna (fruit flan with cream)
Zabaione (custard with Marsala): contains beaten eggs and sugar

Avoid **desserts containing butter, cheese, chocolate, or whole milk.**

ITALIAN DEFENSIVE DINING TIPS

Here are ten tips for anyone who wants to stay on a healthful eating plan while eating Italian food:

1. Call ahead to your favorite Italian dining spot and ask them to prepare *risotto* (rice) and seafood with a little olive oil instead of butter. Follow this dish with a mixed salad, and you have the fixings for a delicious meal.
2. Avoid drinking wine and other alcoholic beverages;

they lower your blood sugar and your resistance to overeating.

3. For your *pasta* choose red sauce made with tomatoes, vegetables, spices, and maybe a little olive oil rather than the white sauces that contain cream, butter, and cheese.
4. Order the appetizer size of *pasta* or soup and a salad for your entire meal.
5. Order vegetarian *pizza* as your entrée. If you're a four-piece *pizza* person, cut two slices in half and add a salad to your meal; you'll be surprised how easy it is to trick your brain into thinking you're eating more.
6. If you are served portions that are too large, ask for a "people bag" at the beginning of a meal. Wrap up the half you don't want to eat and it won't be staring you in the face, asking to be eaten.
7. Use Italian pepper flakes on your food; the tastier food is, the less you eat. The milder it is, the more you want.
8. Enjoy a cup of hot tomato juice, as a snack, with a couple of Italian breadsticks.
9. If your stomach is full, but your mouth is hungry, munch on the heel of Italian bread, two or three crunchy breadsticks, or a crunchy salad.
10. Enjoy a hot cup of *cappuccino* made with nonfat milk and topped with chocolate. Close your eyes and pretend you're eating a rich, creamy dessert.

Italian Phrases

If you are fortunate enough to find yourself in Italy, show these Italian phrases to the waiter so you can enjoy delicious Italian dishes while staying on your diet.

1. **I'd like a glass of mineral water.**
   Gradirei un bicchiere d'acqua minerale per favore.

2. **Please bring me a vegetable *antipasto*.**
   Per favore mi porti un antipasto di verdure.

3. **Please bring me some Italian bread without oil or butter.**
   Per favore mi porti del pane italiano senz' olio o burro.

4. **I'd like a plate of *pasta*, any type of noodle that isn't made with egg, topped with no-oil marinara sauce, please.**
   Gradirei un piatto di pasta di qualunque tipo che non contenga uova, e con salsa alla marinara senz' olio, per favore.

5. **Please bring me a chicken or meat dish made without oil.**
   Per favore mi dia del pollo o carne preparati senz' olio.

6. **I'd like whatever type of fresh fish you have, broiled, poached, or grilled.**
   Gradirei qualunque tipo di pesce fresco che avete, arrostito, affogato, o alla griglia.

7. **I would like a *pizza* with no meat, plenty of tomato sauce, and vegetables, but go light with the cheese and oil. Thanks.**
   Gradirei una pizza senza carne, con molta salsa di pomodoro e verdura, ma con poco formaggio ed olio. Grazie.

8. **I'd like a mixed green salad with Italian vinaigrette dressing on the side. Thank you.**
   Gradirei una insalata mista e condimento a base di aceto separato. Grazie.

9. **For dessert I would like some fresh fruit and a decaffeinated *cappuccino* made with nonfat milk and topped with chocolate.**
   Per dolce gradirei della frutta fresca e un cappuccino senza caffeina fatto con latte scremato e un po' di cioccolata sopra.

10. Bring me the check, please.
Mi porti il conto, grazie!

THE BOTTOM LINE

Now that you know what to order and how to have your food prepared, once "forbidden" foods such as *pizza, pasta*, bread, rice, beans, and potatoes are now part of your healthful eating plan.

Today, the entire family can stay on their diets while eating in Italian restaurants. *Pizza* and other fast foods can be tailored to fit a low-fat diet if you omit the cheese and go heavy with the healthful toppings. *Pizza* is readily available, it's comforting, delicious, reasonably priced, and it's good for you too.

Mexican food, which can also be incorporated into a healthful diet, is the subject of our next chapter. *Buòn appetito!* (Enjoy yourself!)

Chapter 7

▲

MEXICAN FOODS

MOST people have misconceptions about Mexican food, conjuring up thoughts of plates overflowing with fat, calories, and cholesterol. If you need to increase the fiber in your diet, lose weight, limit fats, avoid sugar, salt, or meat, you'll be happy to know that Mexican foods and their variations can be converted into healthful meals.

REGIONAL MEXICAN COOKING

Mexican food is a combination of ingredients and cooking ideas that came from the conquistadors of Spain and the Aztec Indians who lived where Mexico City is today. The foods we obtained from these people thousands of years ago—corn, tomatoes, chilies, chicken, and beans—are still the most important ingredients used to make traditional dishes in Mexico today.

Spanish Food

Spanish foods are a merging of Mediterranean and Italian influences. Their dishes contain a lot of seafood and rice, but not many beans. Saffron is often used to season the food, and olive oil is the chosen fat for cooking and dressing salads.

Mexican-Style Foods

Mexican food, Spanish food, and their American takeoffs are available in restaurants throughout the United States today. Tex-Mex and Southwestern cooking have their own unique styles.

Tex-Mex is a combination of the spicy styles of West Texas and Mexico. It consists of foods such as *tacos, enchiladas, flautas, burritos, chiles rellenos*, rice, and beans made with fresh peppers and dried chilies.

Southwestern food is upscale Mexican/American food—California style. More salads are on the menu, and everything is made fresh. Thus it's easy to convert items on southwestern menus into healthful alternatives. Olive oil is generally used for cooking. Spices, hot peppers, and lime wedges add flavor, so you don't need salt. Cumin, cilantro, coriander, oregano, and chili peppers are used to flavor the food, and nothing is fried.

Lard

Lard and corn oil are the fats most commonly used for cooking Mexican and Mexican-style foods, but nobody wants to eat beans or anything else made with lard these days, because they know what animal fat does to their arteries. Fortunately, every Mexican recipe can be modified by substituting corn or one of the other good oils for lard, nonfat milk for cream, and salsa for sour cream and salad dressing. Other Mexican dishes can be made more healthful by changing the cooking technique (poaching, steaming, barbecuing, or broiling instead of frying).

HEALTHFUL MEXICAN MENU

Whenever I think of healthful Mexican food I remember a client of mine who wanted to hire a mariachi band and throw himself a birthday fiesta, but whose friends were all on special eating regimens. I suggested he go to his favorite neighborhood Mexican restaurant and ask the owners to convert the foods he preferred into healthful alternatives.

They suggested he start the fiesta off with oven-roasted *tortilla* chips and a large bowl of *salsa* for dipping. The *salsa* he served was made with chilies, cilantro (Mexican parsley), tomatoes, onions, lemon or lime juice, and no salt or oil.

In addition to the *frijoles de la olla* (pot beans), Spanish rice (made without oil) and steamed corn *tortillas* were served on the side. Corn *tortillas*, unlike flour ones, don't contain lard.

The *tamales* were made with a spiced meat or vegetable filling rolled in *masa de harina* (corn mixture), wrapped in *hojas* (corn husks), and steamed. *Burritos*, chicken, and "select" beef *tamales* were also served. To make them succulent, yet healthful, the leftover liquid from cooking the chicken and beef was added to the *masa harina* instead of lard. The *burritos* were filled with fresh-cooked turkey, chicken, and select beef. On a Mexican menu, these are the leanest meats.

My client next served a bowl of watermelon *agua fresca* (watermelon juice with water and chunks of fresh fruit). This is a healthful, refreshing drink everyone can enjoy. For dessert he served strawberry sherbet in addition to an assortment of fresh and dried fruits.

MEXICAN FAST FOOD

There is a revolution going on in the fast-food industry. All fast food is no longer the same. Even though it's a meal you can pick up and eat quickly, it doesn't have to be unhealthful.

Many restaurant chains serve nutritious Mexican fast foods—delicious chicken *tostados* and beef-and-bean *burritos*. Just make sure to order food that isn't deep-fried and request heated corn *tortillas* with your order.

Actually, once you know what to order, you can turn every restaurant into a healthful fast-food spot. Pick up a dinner salad and a side order of beans or vegetables with heated *tortillas* and *picante* sauce for a fast and nutritious meal. Another idea is to order *fajitas* made from chicken (without the skin, of course), pork, strip steak, or another comparable lean beef. If you add an extra order of steamed corn *tortillas*, one order of *fajitas* is usually enough for two people.

For a quick *quesadilla* to take the edge off your appetite when you're at home or the office, sprinkle a corn *tortilla* with cheese and a dash of *salsa*. Add tomato, onion, chilies, and red, yellow, or green peppers. Heat open-faced in the microwave or toaster oven, fold the *tortilla* in half, and enjoy.

Tacos

Tacos are relatively low in calories, and when made with one of the more healthful oils, they're as nutritious as a good sandwich. The *tortillas* used for soft *tacos* are usually made with corn oil. Some fast-food restaurants such as Taco Bell, however, use coconut oil, a saturated fat, to fry the corn *tortillas* used to make *tacos*, *tostados*, and cinnamon *crispas*—fried *tortillas* with a sugary topping. They make what seems like a healthful version of a *burrito* with a steamed flour *tortilla* to hold the ingredients together, but remember that most flour *tortillas* contain lard—

another saturated fat. I hope, in the near future, they make heated corn *tortillas* a health-conscious option.

Here are the calorie counts for some of the typical Mexican-style fast foods. But when it comes to good health, remember: there's more to think about than calories.

Taco Bell Menu Items

	Calories
Tostada	179
Taco	186
Beefy *tostada*	291
Bean *burrito*	343
Combination *burrito*	404
Enchirito	454
Burrito Supreme	457
Beef *burrito*	466

Jack-in-the-Box Menu Items

	Calories
Regular *taco*	191
Super *taco*	288
Taco salad	377

Chicken

For Mexican-style chicken, take a look at the El Pollo Loco restaurants springing up in little shopping malls throughout the United States. At Pollo Loco you can order char-broiled chicken that has been marinated in a combination of fresh fruit juices. The chicken is served with fresh *salsa*, corn on the cob, and corn *tortillas*. Lean-beef tacos and burritos are also on the menu. Avoid their potato salad and coleslaw, however; they are loaded with mayonnaise.

In most fast-food spots the food is made to order, so you can end up with a relatively low-fat and delicious fast meal if you remember these points:

- Make sure the restaurant cooks with one of the better oils, such as corn, canola, soy, olive, or safflower.
- Ask for salad dressings, *guacamole*, sour cream, and cheese on the side, so you're in charge of how much of these condiments you eat.
- Avoid eating the foods at chains like Taco Bell and Jack-in-the-Box that contain highly saturated fats.

Vegetarian Fast Food

Naturally Fast, in West Los Angeles, California, is an example of one of the many restaurants serving healthful and delicious authentic vegetarian fast foods. You can eat there or take out. They offer soups, salads, sandwiches, Mexican entrées, desserts, soft-serve nonfat yogurt, and cold drinks containing no sugar. **Their American Heart Association–approved items are cholesterol free, sugar free, and low in sodium.** Their food is made without sacrificing taste or quality. I predict that more Mexican fast-food menus will look like theirs in the future. Hearts (♥) indicate healthful dishes.

▲

NATURALLY FAST MENU

Entrees

1. **Enchilada Pie**
   Enchilada sauce, organic corn tortillas, jack and cheddar cheese, green chiles, tomatoes, cilantro and onions.
2. **Enchilada Pie Plate♥**
   Enchilada pie, salsa, chips & green salad.

♥-Approved by the American Heart Association

3. **Spaghetti and Sauce♥**
   Spaghetti sauce, slimetti noodles with parmesan cheese.
4. **Spaghetti and Sauce♥**
   Spaghetti sauce, roll (whole wheat, or whole wheat onion poppyseed) and green salad.
5. **Lasagne**
   Lasagne sauce, artichoke noodles, ricotta cheese, mozzarella cheese, parmesan cheese and spinach.
6. **Lasagne Plate**
   Lasagne, roll (whole wheat, or whole wheat onion poppyseed) and green salad.
7. **Steamed Vegetables♥**
8. **Steamed Vegetable Plate♥**
   Steamed vegetables, organic brown rice, marinated organic tofu, roll and your choice of sauce (mushroom gravy, jambalaya♥ or marinara♥).
9. **Tofu Combo**
   Marinated organic tofu, organic brown rice and your choice of sauce.
10. **Red Tamale♥**
    Cornmeal, tofu, sunflower seeds, chili, corn oil and salt.
11. **Green Tamale**
    Cornmeal, jack cheese, green chili, corn oil and salt.
12. **Burrito**
    Tannour Bread (whole wheat flour, vegetable oil, honey and sea salt), beans, cheddar cheese, salad base and salsa.
13. **Tostada**
    Organic corn tortilla, beans, cheddar cheese, salad base, sour cream, salsa, green onions and black olives.

Burgers

All burgers are served on "Goodstuff" eggless buns.
All mayonnaise is eggless.

1. **Vegetable and Cheese**
   Onions, green peppers, mushrooms, tomatoes, sprouts, cheddar cheese, ketchup and mayo.
2. **Tempeh♥**
   Tempeh cutlet, tomatoes, sprouts, onions, mayo and tahini sauce.

♥-Approved by the American Heart Association

3. **Falafel♥**
   Falafel patty, cucumber, cabbage, tomatoes, onions, mayo and tahini sauce.
4. **Nature♥**
   Mixture of grains and vegetables in a patty with tomatoes, sprouts, mayo, BBQ sauce and dressing.
5. **Tofu♥**
   Tofu patty, sprouts, tomatoes, mayo, mustard, relish and BBQ sauce.
6. **Veggie BBQ**
   Soy protein marinated in a natural BBQ sauce.

Stuffed Potatoes

1. **Mushrooms and Cheese**
   Sauteed mushrooms, cheddar cheese, sour cream, and green onions.
2. **Broccoli and Cheese**
   Broccoli, tomatoes and cheddar cheese.
3. **Mexican**
   Salsa, cheddar cheese, black olives, sour cream and green onions.
4. **Baked Potato**
   Butter, sour cream, and green onions.

Side Orders

Organic Brown Rice♥
Mushroom Gravy♥
Jambalaya Sauce♥
Marinara Sauce♥
Marinated Organic Tofu♥
Veggie BBQ♥
Salsa (2 oz.)
Chips
Salsa (4 oz.) & Chips
Avocado
Cheese
Salad Dressing

▼

♥-Approved by the American Heart Association

How to Be a Healthy Vegetarian

For people to be healthy, they need to obtain the twenty-two different kinds of amino acids that perform essential functions in their bodies. Animal protein contains all of these essential amino acids. Vegetables, grains, legumes (dried peas, beans, and peanuts), nuts, seeds, eggs, and dairy products, however, do not contain nine of the necessary amino acids.

Our bodies can reconstruct thirteen of the amino acids we need from the foods we eat, but we cannot manufacture the remaining nine. For that reason, they are called the ***nine essential amino acids***, and they must be supplied in their final form from the protein foods we eat.

Every cuisine can be adapted to a healthful vegetarian diet if you combine foods plentiful in some of the amino acids with different foods abundant in the others. Appropriate combinations are called ***complementary proteins***.

Mexican dishes can be combined to make healthful vegetarian entrées containing the nine essential amino acids. Traditional Mexican dishes, such as *pisto* (eggs with vegetables) or beans with rice, corn, or wheat, are examples of complementary proteins. If you need to avoid meat, for whatever reason, it's important to combine your foods properly; a haphazard vegetarian diet doesn't provide the nine essential amino acids you need.

Three Easy Alternatives

- Combine legumes (dried peas, beans, and peanuts) with grains such as rice, bread, or anything made with flour.
- Combine legumes with nuts and seeds.
- Combine eggs or dairy products with any vegetable protein such as sunflower seeds, corn, rice, or wheat.

✓TO CHOOSE

To know which foods to order and avoid in Mexican restaurants, use this Mexican-Style Menu Command. It tells which fattening dishes to avoid and which low-calorie dishes to choose.

Drinks (Bebidas)

Agua mineral (mineral water): drink four to six 8-ounce glasses of bottled water a day. Do not drink fresh water in Mexico, unless accustomed to it.
Atole (*masa de harina*, cornmeal, a little sugar, milk, and vanilla flavoring
Café con leche (coffee with milk): not fattening if nonfat milk is used
Café de olla (coffee): made in an earthenware pot, comes with *piloncillo*, cones of rich dark sugar
Cerveza mexicana (Mexican beer): drink in moderation, diet permitting
Champagne *margarita*: diet permitting alcohol, drink in moderation
Leche descremada caliente (hot steamed milk): request nonfat
Ponche tropical (tropical fruit punch): mostly juice with a little sugar
Sangría (soda water, red wine, oranges, and limes): drink only occasionally, diet permitting alcohol
Té (tea)
Té de hiervas (herb tea)
Watermelon *agua fresca* (watermelon juice with water): can be made with bottled water

***Choose* refreshing juice drinks that contain a lot of water.**
***BEST BETS: Agua mineral*, watermelon *agua fresca*, or *café con leche* (request nonfat milk).**

✓ To Choose

Appetizers (Antojitos or Tapas)

Almejas al vapor (steamed clams)
Ceviche (marinated raw fish served with vegetables and lime)
Coctel mariscos con limón (shellfish cocktail with lemon)
Jícama fresca (*jícama* appetizer with squeezed lime): can also be a dessert
Nachos (*tostada* chips topped with cheese and chilies)
Pescado espada y melón en brocheta (skewered fish and cantaloupe)
Tamalitos (little *tamales*): order if they are made without lard
Tostada chips (triangular pieces of crisp-fried corn *tortillas* served with *salsa*): order ones that have been oven-roasted instead of fried

***Choose salsa* and other healthy low-fat appetizers such as yogurt-based spreads and dips made from pureed vegetables.**
BEST BETS: ceviche* and *tamalitos

Soups (Sopas)

Caldo michi (fish soup)
Gazpacho (chopped raw vegetables such as tomatoes, cucumbers, onion, and green peppers)
Potage mexicano (Mexican boiled dinner): beans, carrots, green beans, and beef or chicken
Sopa de albóndigas (meatball and vegetable soup)
Sopa de fideos (vermicelli soup): contains noodles, beef stock, tomatoes, and onions
Sopa de frijol (black bean soup): order when made with oil instead of lard

✓ To Choose

Sopa de habas (dried fava bean soup)
Sopa de legumbres (vegetable soup)
Sopa de tomate y arroz (tomato rice soup)
Sopa de tortilla (*tortilla* soup): healthy when made with oil instead of lard

***Choose* chicken- or tomato-based soups.**
***BEST BETS: sopa de albóndigas* or gazpacho**

Breads (Pan), Beans (Fríjoles), and Rice (Arroz)

Arroz con azafrán (simple saffron rice)
Arroz con langosta (rice and lobster): a side dish or an entire meal
Arroz mexicana (Mexican rice)
Arroz negro (black rice): the liquid from cooking black beans is added to white rice
Fríjoles de la olla (pot beans): whole beans (black, pinto, or kidney) made without bacon fat or lard.
Fríjoles meneados (bean puree): beans blended *en líquido* (in liquid)
Fríjoles negros (black beans)
Lentejas guisadas (stewed lentils)
Posole (white corn kernels treated with lime and made with lean pork)
Tortillas de maiz (corn *tortillas*): a thin flat cake made of blue or yellow cornmeal

***Choose* heated corn *tortillas* made without fat.**
BEST BET: tortillas de maiz

Salads (Ensaladas) and Vegetables (Legumbres)

Berenjena al horno (baked eggplant)
Calabacines (chopped zucchini)

✓TO CHOOSE

Calabacines en vinagre (marinated zucchini)
Carne a la vinagreta (marinated beef salad)
Coliflor (cauliflower): one cup contains 28 calories
Elote (ear of fresh corn): contains 70 calories
Ensalada de chayote (salad with squash): a fruit eaten usually as a vegetable
Ensalada de ejotes (green bean salad)
Ensalada de lechuga romana (romaine lettuce salad): the darker green the lettuce, the more nutrition it contains.
Ensalada de verduras (vegetable salad)
Escalibadas (grilled vegetables): traditionally cooked over an open fire
Maiz guisado sin mantequilla (stewed corn): made without butter
Pesadumbre (marinated vegetable salad)
Pico de gallo (jícama salad)

Choose **raw or steamed vegetables or fruit salads marinated in small amounts of polyunsaturated or monounsaturated oils.**
BEST BETS: Ensalada de lechuga romana **(substitute *salsa* or chili sauce for salad dressing and save 120 calories)**

Snacks (Tapas)

Quesadilla (corn *tortilla* filled with cheese and sometimes vegetables)
Taco (corn *tortilla* folded around chicken, lean beef or pork, lettuce, tomato, and a little cheese)

Choose **low-fat snacks that are filling but not fattening.**
BEST BET: Quesadillas **made with soft corn *tortillas***

✓ To Choose

Entrées (Platos Principales)

Albóndigas (big light meatballs flecked with rice and seasoned with mint)
Arroz con pescado (rice with fish)
Arroz con pollo (chicken with rice)
Burritos (*tortillas* filled with combinations of beans, cheese, and meat): request a corn *tortilla* or lard-free flour one
Carne asada barbacoa (roasted or barbecued meat): make sure it's lean
Carne desilada (shredded beef)
Carnitas (browned pork bits): boiled and then broiled, so they are lean
Chili con carne (beef with chili): make sure the beef is lean
Chile macho de puerco (pork in hot chili sauce): if made with oil instead of lard
Enchiladas de pollo o carne (*tortillas* that have been filled with chicken or meat, dipped into sauce, topped with a moderate amount of cheese, and heated in the oven): if fried in lard, avoid them
Fajitas (little belts—onions, bell peppers, chicken, beef, or shrimp, cooked quickly in a little oil): eat with heated corn *tortillas*
Filete miñon (filet mignon): 3½ ounces equals 1 serving
Guisado de pollo (chicken stew): if made with oil instead of butter
Huachinango en la parrilla (broiled red snapper)
Huevos con camarónes (eggs with shrimp): eliminate one egg yolk and request Pam or oil instead of butter
Huevos con tomate (tomato and eggs): eliminate one egg yolk and request Pam cooking spray or 1 teaspoon oil instead of butter
Huevos en chile colorado (eggs cooked in red chili sauce):

✓TO CHOOSE

eliminate one egg yolk and request Pam or oil instead of butter

Huevos en chile verde (eggs cooked in green chili sauce): eliminate one egg yolk and request Pam or oil instead of butter

Huevos rancheros (country-style eggs): eliminate one egg yolk and request Pam or oil instead of lard

Huevos revueltos rancheros (scrambled eggs ranch style): eliminate one egg yolk and request Pam or 1 tablespoon polyunsaturated or monounsaturated oil

Langosta al vapor (steamed lobster)

Paella (classic seafood dish seasoned with saffron, includes rice, chicken, red peppers, tomatoes, and peas): a typically Spanish dish made with olive oil

Patas de cangrejo al vapor (crab legs steamed)

Pavo (turkey)

Pescado con salsa de perejil (fish in parsley sauce)

Pescado con vino blanco (fish in white wine): request oil instead of butter

Pescado en salsa de ají (fish in chili sauce)

Pescado Veracruz (red snapper Veracruz)

Picadillo (ground meat)

Pisto (scrambled eggs with vegetables): eliminate one egg yolk and request oil instead of butter

Pollo con naranjas (chicken with oranges)

Pollo con repollo al horno (baked chicken and cabbage)

Pollo en mole verde (chicken in green chili sauce): order if made with oil instead of lard

Pollo en salsa de chile ancho (chicken in mild red chili sauce): order if made with oil instead of lard

Quesadillas (cheese and chili filling inside a corn *tortilla*): request a heated, not fried, *tortilla*

✓TO CHOOSE

Tacos (meat filling, garnish, and spicy sauce inside a corn *tortilla*)
Tamales (*masa de harina*, specially prepared corn around filling): healthful when made with liquid from cooking the filling and no lard; a meal in themselves
Torta (meat sandwich in a big French roll painted with a thin layer of beans, filled with meat, lettuce, and tomato)
Tortilla de huevos (Mexican omelet): ask the chef to eliminate one egg yolk
Tostadas (flat *tortilla* with beans, shredded lettuce, and garnish)
Zarzuela (shellfish with a light sauce): named after an operetta

Choose* dishes with fish, shellfish, chicken, lean pork, or select beef prepared in red or green hot sauce. Other good choices are steamed *tamales* made without lard, *enchiladas, tacos*, and *burritos* made with corn *tortillas
***BEST BETS: langosta al vapor* (steamed lobster), *pescado Veracruz* (red snapper Veracruz), or *pavo* (turkey)**

Sauces (Salsas)

Aderezo para ensalada (salad dressing): ingredients vary—just make sure it's made with one of the healthful oils, and order it on the side
Salsa (finely chopped vegetables, chilies, and tomatoes): spices up any dish
Salsa de chile rojo (red chili sauce)
Salsa de chile verde (green chili sauce)
Salsa enchilada (*enchilada* sauce—red sauce of mild chili pulp, a little salt, and seasonings)

✓TO CHOOSE

Salsa jalapeña (hot relish made of jalapeño peppers, onions, and tomatoes; can be made with red tomatoes or green ones)
Salsa mexicana (Mexican red chili sauce)
Salsa picante estilo mexicano (Mexican hot sauce)
Salsa tobasco (Tabasco sauce): the hottest red sauce
Salsa verde (green sauce): hotter than the red
Taco sauce (red or green tomatoes, chilies, vinegar, onions, and seasonings)
Tomatillos (green tomato sauce)

***Choose* sauces made from red or green tomatoes: sauces made from vine-ripened tomatoes taste best.**
***BEST BETS: Salsa* or *taco* sauce**

Desserts (Postres)

Arroz con leche (rice pudding): not too fattening if you don't eat too much
Frigo (sherbet): ½ cup contains approximately 94 calories
Frutos frescos (fresh fruits)
Guanaba (a fruit eaten fresh): it tastes a little like kiwi
Guayabate (sweet, firm, jamlike paste made from guavas; also called *membrillo*)
Helado de jugo de frutos (ice cream made with fruit juice): some varieties are low-fat
Manzana asada (baked apple): usually baked with cinnamon and a little honey
Postre de higos chumbos (fresh prickly pear dessert)

***Choose* fresh or dried fruit and sherbet.**
***BEST BET: helado de jugo de frutas* (ice cream made with fruit juice)**

⊘ To Avoid

Drinks

Café con leche (coffee with milk): made with whole milk
Champurrado (chocolate atole): made with whole milk and chocolate
Coctel de tequila (tequila cocktail): contains grenadine and white tequila
Leche con chocolate (cocoa made with milk)
Margarita (cocktail): contains tequila, Triple Sec or Cointreau, and lime juice
Margarita chablis (wine margarita): occasionally, diet permitting
Piña colada (coconut, alcoholic drink)
Rompope (Mexican eggnog): egg-based Mexican liqueur blended with orange juice and gin
Sangrita (tequila drink with oranges, limes, onion, and chilies): often served with tequila as a chaser
Tequila sling (tequila, lime, and sparkling water)
Tequila y naranja (tequila sunrise): orange juice, white tequila, and grenadine

Avoid **beverages containing whole milk, half and half, cream, ice cream, and nondairy creamers. Avoid alcoholic beverages such as tequila, Kahlúa, Grand Marnier, Cointreau, and cream liqueurs, unless you can afford the sugar and calories. If you drink them, do so only occasionally.**

Appetizers

Cacahuetes (peanuts with chili powder): nuts are high in fat and these nuts are covered with salt
Chalupas, chonitas, garnaches, gorditas, and *sopes* (round,

⊘ TO AVOID

boat-shaped *masa* dough deep-fried in lard; fillings vary)

Chili con queso (Mexican fondue): melted cheese with chilies

Chiles rellenos (stuffed peppers): usually contain a lot of cheese

Guacamole (a concoction of crushed avocado): although a monounsaturated fat, avocados are high in calories; eat moderate amounts only—one medium avocado contains 350 calories

Refried bean dip (refried beans topped with cheese and *taco* sauce): usually contains lard

Taquito (a miniature version of a *taco*): usually fried and covered with *guacamole*

***Avoid* fried appetizers. Limit mayonnaise and sour cream–based dips.**

Soups

Cocido (soup and meat in a single dish): too fatty

Menudo (tripe and hominy soup)

Sopa de aguacate (avocado soup): contains avocados and cream

Sopa de arroz con jamón (rice soup with ham)

Sopa de bolitas de tortilla (*tortilla*-ball soup): contains lard

Sopa de elote (corn soup): contains butter and cream

Sopa de flor de calabaza (squash-blossom soup): contains butter

Sopa seca de fideos (Mexican vermicelli *au gratin*): contains lard and cheese—remember, cheese is mainly fat

Sopa sonorense (Sonoran corn soup): contains whipping cream

⊘ To Avoid

***Avoid* salty soups and soups containing cream or butter.**

Beans and Breads

Bolillos mexicanos (sweet bread): contains too much sugar
Cuernos (croissants): too much butter
Hojaldre (puff paste roll): contains a lot of butter
Pan de elote (cornbread): contains lard or butter
Pan dulce (sweet buns): usually contains butter
Rosca de tres reyes (three kings' bread): usually contains butter
Tortillas de harina (flour *tortillas*): usually contain lard

***Avoid* flour tortillas, unless they do not contain lard.**

Salads and Vegetables

Acelgas con crema (creamed Swiss chard): contains heavy cream
Chili rajas con crema (chili strips with cream): contains heavy cream
Churros de plátano (banana fritters): fried in fat
Ensalada de noche buena (Christmas Eve salad): loaded with mayonnaise
Ensalada de camarón (shrimp salad): contains sour cream and mayonnaise
Ensalada rusa (Russian salad): loaded with mayonnaise
Plátanos parrillo (broiled bananas): loaded with butter

***Avoid* salads in sour cream and mayonnaise-based dressings.**

Snacks

⊘ To Avoid

Flautas (*tortillas*, filled, rolled, and fried)
Gorditas ("little fat ones"—calorie-laden snacks, fat cakes of fried *masa*, sometimes split and stuffed with beans, meat, and cheese)
Tacos de frijoles con chorizo (tacos with beans and sausage): sausage is fatty and contains nitrates
Taquitos (little *tacos* rolled, fried, and smothered with *guacamole*)

***Avoid* fatty snacks.**

Entrées

Birria de chivo (goat meat): too fatty
Bistec de ternera (veal chop): too fatty
Chiles rellenos (stuffed peppers dipped in batter and fried)
Chiles rellenos con queso (chilies stuffed with cheese)
Costillas de res (short ribs of beef): too fatty
Lengua de res al horno (baked beef tongue): all organ meats contain a lot of cholesterol
Manchamanteles ("tablecloth stainer," a combination of chicken and pork in *mole* sauce) too fatty and sugary—contains chocolate
Pato (duck): too fatty
Pescado con guacamole (fish with avocado sauce): avocado is high in calories
Pescado nacional (fried red snapper): lard is usually used for cooking this dish
Pollo con chorizo (chicken with highly seasoned Spanish link sausage)
Sesos con jitomate (brains with tomato): all organ meats are high in cholesterol

⊘ TO AVOID

Sopa seca de tortillas (*tortilla* dry soup): casserole containing cream, lard, and cheese
Taco de lengua (tongue): high in cholesterol

***Avoid* organ meats and fried entrées—anything made with cream, butter, or lard.**

Sauces

Guacamole (avocado dip): high in calories, particularly when mayonnaise is added
Mayonesa (mayonnaise): fatty—contains egg yolk and oil
Mole (a sauce usually used with chicken or turkey): contains lard and usually Mexican chocolate
Puré de plátano (banana puree): contains milk, sugar, banana, and butter
Salsa de hongos (mushroom sauce): contains butter
Salsa española (a brown sauce): contains butter and ham or bacon

***Avoid* fatty and sugary sauces.**

Desserts

Budín de chocolate (Mexican chocolate pudding): contains eggs, sugar, and whole milk
Buñuelos de plátano (banana fritters): contain shortening
Campechanas (sugar-glazed flaky pastries): contain milk, sugar, and shortening
Capirotada, salsa de Cuervo (Mexican bread pudding served with tequila sauce)
Chongos zamoranos (cheese pudding in syrup): contains milk, cheese rennet, and sugary syrup

⊘TO AVOID

Churros (fried batter cakes): contain oil, sugar, and eggs
Coda (coconut custard): contains eggs, whipping cream, and sugar
Crepas de cajeta (crepes with candy and sauce)
Empanadas (turnovers): deep-fried in shortening
Flan (caramel pudding): contains sugar, whole milk, eggs, and 303 calories per serving
Jericalla (custard): contains sugar, whole milk, and eggs
Molletes (sweet rolls): contain sugar, whole milk, and shortening
Nieve frita con salsa de coco (deep-fried ice cream with chocolate sauce)
Pan de muerto (bread of the dead): contains butter
Pan dulce (sweet bread): contains butter and sugar
Sopapillas (fritters): contain lard, honey, and shortening for frying
Tamales de caramelo (caramel *tamales*)
Tamales de dulce (sweet *tamales*): filled with fruits such as apricots or peaches and usually too much sugar
Tortada (mango tart): contains butter and sugar

***Avoid* desserts made with butter, shortening, whole milk, and cream.**

MEXICAN DEFENSIVE DINING TIPS

Here are ten tips for anyone who wants to stay on a diet while eating in Mexican restaurants:

1. Call in advance and ask the chef for special food preparation if your diet requires it. More often than not, you will be accommodated; they will leave the salt out

of your soup, the oil out of your sauce, and the lard out of your beans. If the chef will not adapt to your needs, order à la carte and assemble an appropriate meal yourself.

2. Avoid eating the chips if they are fried in coconut oil or if they are too salty. Request oven-roasted chips instead, and limit the number you eat. Chips are addicting; if they tempt you to fill up before the main course arrives, ask the waiter to remove them from your table.
3. Order a fresh vegetable appetizer and *salsa* for dipping or heated corn *tortillas* as a substitute for chips.
4. Select *gazpacho*, bean, or vegetable soups instead of creamed soups that are high in fat.
5. Make wise menu choices. Avoid items that are *frito* (fried), *refrito* (refried), *dulce* (sweet), and *grande* (big).
6. Order cooked beans, heated corn *tortillas*, and a salad as your whole meal.
7. Request all Mexican dishes with sour cream, cheese toppings, and *guacamole* on the side.
8. Substitute a side order of Mexican or Spanish rice for refried beans made with lard and you'll save 50 calories.
9. When you are particularly hungry, order a chicken *taco* in a steamed corn *tortilla*, and ask for extra *tortillas* on the side. Split the *taco* filling among the three *tortillas*, sprinkle them with sauce, and you have a filling meal.
10. And now, my favorite tip of all. Most Tex-Mex, Southwestern, Mexican, and Spanish desserts don't fit dieters' requirements. They're fattening because they're loaded with sugar and fat. Fortunately desserts offer a diner flexibility—they can be skipped. Skip them!

Spanish Phrases

When the menu is in Spanish and the waiters don't speak English, show the waiter these phrases:

1. **I want my food made without salt, lard, butter, or cream. Please bring all sauces on the side.**
   Quiero mi comida preparada sin sal, sin grasa, y sin crema. Por favor, traiga las salsas por separado.

2. **I would like an order of oven-roasted *tortilla* chips, without salt and made without fat, please.**
   Quiero una orden de tortilla chips sin sal y sin grasa, doradas al horno, por favor.

3. **I would like a bowl of soup prepared without salt and without cream.**
   Quiero un plato de sopa hecha sin sal y sin crema.

4. **I would like a green salad with vinaigrette dressing on the side.**
   Quiero una ensalada verde con aderezo de vinagre sin aceite por separado.

5. **I would like to have an order of heated corn *tortillas*.**
   Quiero una orden de tortillas de maiz calientes.

6. **Please bring me fish, chicken, turkey, lean beef, or lean pork (choose one of the following cooking methods):**
   a. mesquite-grilled
   b. dry-broiled
   c. barbecued
   d. steamed
   Por favor, traigame una orden de pescado, pollo, pavo, carne desgrasada, o carne de puerco del lomo:
   a. al carbón
   b. asada a la parrilla
   c. adobada
   d. al vapor

7. **I would like a fresh green or yellow vegetable steamed and prepared without butter or cream.**
   Quiero una orden de verduras frescas, verdes o amarillas, preparadas al vapor sin mantequilla o crema.

8. **I would like some fresh fruit sherbet for my dessert.**
Quiero una helado de agua de fruta para mi postre.

9. **Please bring me a cup of coffee (decaffeinated) with nonfat milk, no sugar.**
Por favor, traigame una taza de café (decafinado) con leche descremada, sin azucar.

10. **All I need is the check, thank you.**
Todo lo que necesito es la cuenta, muchas gracias.

THE BOTTOM LINE

South-of-the-border cuisines make it possible to eat out while staying on a healthful low-calorie eating plan. Avoid fried foods, order lean meat and lots of fresh vegetables, eliminate lard or shortening, and have your foods cooked with moderate amounts of one of the good oils instead. Order dishes that are light on meat and chicken and heavy on low-calorie, high-fiber toppings such as chopped tomato, onion, shredded lettuce, and *salsa*. Typically Mexican foods such as rice, corn, beans, chilies, and tomatoes are very nutritious.

When you are in a hurry and want a quick Mexican meal, it's easy to pick up delicious food at a healthful fast-food spot—or at any Mexican restaurant, for that matter. (At some restaurants you can FAX your order.) More fast food is being prepared healthfully than ever before. Just make sure to avoid those prepared with coconut oil and beef fat at the typical Mexican fast-food chains.

Now that we've learned how to modify Mexican menus, it should be a breeze when eating one of the most nutritious cuisines, Chinese.

¡Amigos, buen apetito y disfruten mucho! (Eat well, my friends, and enjoy yourselves!)

Chapter 8

▲

CHINESE FOOD

THE Chinese diet is one of the world's most healthful. Asian people believe in *fan-tsai*. This dietary principle helps them obtain about 80 percent of their calories from grain, 10 percent from vegetables, and 10 percent from animal products and fat.

Although Chinese people don't count calories and eat about 20 percent more than Americans, they are on the average 20 percent thinner. And they have less heart disease and less cancer than Americans. Perhaps we should be eating more like the Chinese.

CHINESE REGIONAL COOKING

In the many regions of China, cooking styles such as Cantonese, Mandarin, Peking, Szechuan, and Hunan were created originally because only certain ingredients were available in each area. Today, however, due to improved transportation and the availability of ingredients everywhere, the food throughout China is pretty much the same, with the exception of Cantonese, which is still distinctive.

Cantonese

Cantonese items are easy to adapt to any healthful eating plan; they're simple, not greasy or spicy, but pure. Dishes such as steamed fish and stir-fried beef and vegetables are characterized by brightly colored crisp vegetables, subtle flavors, and clear sauces.

Mandarin

Mandarin is the collective term for Peking, Szechuan, and Hunan cooking. With the exception of duck, which is popular in Peking (also called Beijing), similar ingredients are used in each region. Some cooking styles are spicier than others, however, so you may prefer dishes indigenous to certain regions over the others. Peking is the least spicy, Szechuan is spicier, and Hunan is the spiciest of the three.

Traditional Chinese Dining

An authentic Chinese meal is an artistic presentation that has no main course but combinations of main courses that are shared by everyone. The only dish you have to yourself is your bowl of rice, except when noodles are eaten alone for a light lunch.

Usually, the number of dishes ordered correlates with the number of people dining at the table. The more people eating a meal, the more chance you have for variety. When additional people join your party, the Chinese custom is to request another dish rather than increase the quantity of food that has already been ordered. Chinese people do not like sugary desserts, so they end their meals with fresh fruit instead of rich pastries.

Variety is important to the Chinese in more ways than just the number of dishes ordered. Chinese chefs strive to create dishes that contrast in taste, texture, size, shape, and color. They choose fresh vegetables for their taste and colors that complement one another.

Each dish usually contains ingredients such as mushrooms, bamboo shoots, and water chestnuts that provide at least two of the four textures: crunchiness, smoothness, softness, and tenderness. By seasoning with soy sauce, rice wine, dry or medium sherry, sugar, vinegar, fresh ginger, scallions, garlic, peppers, and chilies, chefs create dishes with sweet, salty, sour, acid, and bitter fragrances.

Most people in China do not drink tea with their meals. They sip soup, instead, throughout the meal, and use it to flavor their rice. Yet tea is closely associated with the Chinese. This is because they drink tea throughout the day—particularly when visitors stop by—at breakfast and between meals, but seldom during a meal.

Chinese-American Food and Customs

Chinese food in America is becoming more authentic because it's easier for American chefs to obtain Chinese ingredients today. The ratio of fat to vegetables and grains is not the same in Chinese-American restaurants, however, as it is in China. In America a person might order fried wonton, barbecued spareribs, crispy duck, and cabbage in cream sauce and think of it as an authentic Chinese meal.

The customs are not traditional in Chinese-American restaurants, either. Americans drink tea, milk, or soda with their meals and order single dishes—dumplings, or perhaps a bowl of Chinese soup—to eat alone. When the meal is over, instead of being satisfied with fresh fruit, many Americans prefer gooey desserts.

Complex Carbohydrates

Many people believe that eating rice or noodles will contribute to weight gain because of the starch, but at only 4 calories per gram that's a misconception. One cup of rice has less than half the calories of one cup of fish, chicken, or beef, which is made up of protein and fat. Complex carbohydrates are energizing, satisfying foods, not fattening ones.

Eat a generous cup of plain steamed white rice or noodles with your meals. Although that amount of rice or noodles contains approximately 190 calories, complex-carbohydrate foods—fruits, vegetables, and grains—are slimming. They contain fewer calories per ounce than animal protein, and they're more filling.

If you feel hungry immediately after eating a Chinese meal, it's probably because you didn't eat enough rice. It would be like eating an American meal without potatoes or bread. But don't get fooled into thinking complex-carbohydrate Chinese dishes that contain added fat such as fried rice and fried noodles are healthful.

Fats and Oils

Fats and oils contain 9 calories per gram—over twice as many calories as complex carbohydrates—and they're not as filling. By eating complex carbohydrates and lean meats, rather than fattier items, you'll feel more satisfied and be less likely to swing between denial and indulgence, which makes you want to diet or binge.

To avoid cholesterol Chinese chefs use tofu (soy bean curd) and add the leanest meats (top sirloin, flank steak, and tenderloin) as condiments—not as the main course. They cook their food in peanut oil, which is 34 percent polyunsaturated, 48 percent monounsaturated, and only 18 percent saturated.

Because lard is used occasionally in Chinese cooking, and can clog your arteries if you eat too much of it too often, make sure it isn't added to your food.

MSG: Chinese Restaurant Syndrome

MSG, the abbreviation for monosodium glutamate, is the flavor enhancer that used to be an important ingredient in Chinese cooking. Some people complained about adverse reactions, including burning sensations in their upper body, migraine headaches, tightness and pressure around their cheeks, jaws, and chest, and occasionally even heart irregularities, so most chefs stopped using it. To be sure it is left out of your food in every Chinese restaurant, remember to say, "*Please, no MSG.*" If you are allergic to MSG ask the waiter if it was added to any of the precooked items that will be used to make your meal. If it was, order something else.

Dim Sum

Dim sum, which means "heart's delight," are delicious buns filled with meat, shrimp, vegetables, egg, sweet fillings, or tofu and are often eaten, unlike other hors d'oeuvres, for brunch and served with a pot of tea or soy milk. In restaurants *dim sum* are usually only available until 2:00 P.M. when dinner preparations get under way.

Occasionally, leftover *dim sum* are eaten for in-between meal snacks, but never for dinner. Avoid salty, greasy, and fried *dim sum*. The steamed or barbecued varieties I recommend are the more delicious, however, so don't feel badly not eating the others.

Chinese Fast Food

Some Chinese fast foods are deep-fried and loaded with sweet-and-sour sauce, while others are healthful. In the larger cities in China, any foods such as cold noodles, beef, or squid that have already been cooked are considered fast foods.

In minimalls throughout America you'll find Chinese-American fast-food dishes such as fried shrimp and chicken, *tempura* vegetables (deep-fried), or sweet-and-sour pork. Don't fool yourself into thinking these takeouts are anything like the foods the Chinese take in for longer life.

▲

The Plum Tree Inn Menu

Depending upon the ingredients and cooking styles you select, a Chinese meal can be extremely healthful or unhealthful. On the menu that follows from the Plum Tree Inn in Santa Monica, California, **I have checked off a variety of delicious dishes for you to choose.** They call for the better cooking techniques, all beginning with the letter *s*, such as stir-frying (*chaw*), sauté-ing (*poh yau*), stewing (*t'ung woh*), and steaming (*jing*).

Mandarin & Szechuan Cuisine

Hot Appetizers
Po Po Plate *Combination Plate for Two*
Fried Shrimp (4)
Vegetable Spring Roll (4)
Spare Ribs, Shanghai Style
Barbecue Spare Ribs (6)
Fried Wonton
Fried Dumplings (8)

√ Steamed Dumpling (8) [request chicken]
√ Skewered Beef (4)
√ Paper Wrapped Chicken (4)
Chicken Roll
Shrimp Toasts (4)

Cold Appetizers
Cured Pork
√ Drunken Chicken
√ Aromatic Beef
Vegetarian Ham
Smoked Fish
√ Jelly Fish
√ Spiced Chinese Cabbage*
Double Delicacy Cold Cuts
Triple Delicacy Cold Cuts
Assorted Cold Cuts
Plum Tree Assorted Cold Cuts
Deluxe Assorted Cold Cuts

Soup
√ Shredded Bean Cake Soup
√ Assorted Wonton Soup
Sizzling Rice Soup
√ Hot and Sour Soup*
√ Assorted Winter Melon Soup
√ Seafood with Bean Curd Soup
√ Bean Curd Spinach Soup
√ Crab Meat Corn Soup
√ Crab Meat Asparagus Soup
√ Crab Meat in Shark's Fin Soup

Sea Food
√ Sauteed Shrimp
Spicy Shrimp with Peanuts*
Shrimp and Cashew Nuts
√ Shrimp and Chinese Peas
√ Sliced Shrimp in Garlic Sauce*

√ = Recommended   * = Spicy

√ Hot Braised Shrimp*
√ Shrimp in Black Bean Sauce
Shrimp with Sizzling Rice
Sweet and Sour Shrimp
√ Lobster in Black Bean Sauce
√ Hot Braised Lobster*
Scallops in Oyster Flavored Sauce
√ Scallops in Garlic Sauce*
√ Abalone with Black Mushrooms
Roast Fish in Brown Sauce
√ Steamed Fish
√ Hot Braised Fish*
Sweet and Sour Fish *Whole*
√ Fish with Garlic Sauce
√ Sea Cucumbers with Shrimp Seeds
√ Braised Sea Cucumbers w/Green Onion
√ Hot Braised Filet of Fish

Fowl

√ Sliced Chicken in Garlic Sauce*
Spicy Diced Chicken with Peanuts*
Chicken with Cashew Nuts
Walnut Chicken
√ Diced Chicken in Tangerine Sauce*
√ Sliced Chicken with Black Mushrooms
Chicken in Sizzling Rice
√ Szechuan Shredded Chicken*
Peking Duck
Crispy Duckling *Half*
Tea Smoked Duck *Half*
Roasted Duck in Brown Sauce *Half*

Pork, Beef & Lamb

Three Ingredient Tastes
Mu Shu Pork
Twice Cooked Pork*
Hot Szechuan Shredded Pork*
Sweet & Sour Pork

√ = Recommended   * = Spicy

√ Beef with Broccoli
√ Beef with Mushrooms
Shredded Pork with Bean Cakes
√ Beef with Chinese Peas
√ Beef with Scallion
√ Hot Sauteed Shredded Beef*
Spicy Sliced Beef with Peanuts*
Lamb with Scallions
Lamb Hunan Style*
Eight Delicacy Ingredients*

Vegetables
√ Mixed Vegetables
√ Mushrooms and Bamboo Shoots
√ Assorted Mushrooms in Oyster Flavored Sauce
√ Baby Bok Choy with Chinese Mushrooms
Chinese Cabbage in Cream Sauce
√ Sauteed Spinach
√ Crab Meat with Mushrooms
√ Hot Spicy Eggplant*
Eggplant in Brown Sauce
√ Bean Curd in Brown Sauce
√ Hot Szechuan Bean Curd*
√ Bean Curd Home Style*
√ Dry Sauteed String Beans

Casseroles
Duck Casseroles
Fish Casseroles*
√ Assorted Casseroles

Fried Rice
Shrimp Fried Rice
Chicken Fried Rice
Pork Fried Rice
Yang Chow Fried Rice
Beef Fried Rice
Vegetable Fried Rice

√ = Recommended * = Spicy

Noodle Dishes

Pan Fried or Soft Noodles [Request soft noodles; they're delicious]

√ Shrimp and Noodles

√ Chicken and Noodles

Shredded Pork and Noodles

√ Beef and Noodles

√ House Special Noodles

√ Vegetables and Noodles

Sauteed Special Rice Cakes

Plum Tree Specialties

√ 1. BEEF WITH SCALLOPS Served on a Sizzling Hot Plate
Sliced Tender Beef Sauteed with Fresh Scallops and Assorted Vegetables in Oyster Flavored Sauce

√ 2. SLICED CHICKEN WITH FRESH MUSHROOMS
Top Choice Fresh Mushrooms with White Meat Chicken [a delicious diet dish]

√ 3. ASSORTED SEAFOOD Served on a Sizzling Hot Plate
Shrimp, Crab Meat, Scallops and Assorted Vegetables Sauteed in Chef's Special Sauce

4. PLUM TREE SPECIAL CHICKEN STRIPS
Served on a Sizzling Hot Plate
Strips of Chicken Sauteed with Vegetables in Brown Sauce

5. LEMON SCALLOPS Served on a Sizzling Hot Plate
Whole Fresh Scallops Fried in Light Batter, Served with our Special Lemon Sauce

√ 6. HOT BRAISED SCALLOPS* Served on a Sizzling Hot Plate
Fresh Scallops Sauteed with Chef's Special Ginger Sauce

√ 7. ROYAL SEAFOOD
Sauteed Scallops, Shrimps and Mixed in a Very Lovely Light Sauce

√ = Recommended * = Spicy

√ 8. FILET OF FISH IN BLACK BEAN SAUCE
Boneless Fresh Fried Fish in our Special Garlic Black Bean Sauce

√ 9. MINCED CHICKEN WITH PINE NUTS*
Minced Chicken Sauteed Spicy Ginger, Garlic Sauce with Pine Nuts

10. PLUM TREE BEEF*
Chunks of Tender Beef Deep Fried and Sauteed with Orange Peel and Scallions in Spicy Sauce

11. CRISPY FISH*
Deep Fried Whole Fish Served in Chef's Special Spicy Sauce

12. SPICY JUMBO SHRIMP*
Tender Shrimp Fried in a Light Batter and Cooked with Chef's Special Spices

13. SWEET & PUNGENT SHRIMP*
Tender Shrimp Fried in a Light Batter and Sauteed in Sweet & Pungent Sauce

14. SWEET & PUNGENT CHICKEN*
Tender Chicken Fried in a Light Batter and Sauteed in Sweet & Pungent Sauce

√ 15. PLUM TREE SHRIMP*
Fresh Sliced Shrimp Sauteed in Plum Tree Special Sauce

√ 16. VEGETABLE DELUXE
Healthy and Light, Perfect Accompaniment to any Dish

√ 17. JADE CHICKEN*
Marinated Chicken Strips Sauteed and Smothered in Seasonal Greens

√ 18. VELVET SHRIMP
Fresh Shrimp Sauteed in Fluffy Eggwhite with Chef's Special Sauce

√ 19. MINCED LOBSTER*
Fine Minced Lobster Cooked in the Szechuan Style, Served with Endive

√=Recommended   *=Spicy

√ 20. FAMOUS BARBECUE CHICKEN SALAD
Shredded Barbecue Chicken, Lettuce with Sweet Ginger, Mixed with Toasted Rice Noodles

21. LEMON CHICKEN
Boneless Chicken Lightly Breaded and Pan Fried, Served with Our Special Lemon Sauce

√ 22. KON PAO LOBSTER*
Chunks of Lobster Meat Sauteed with Green Onion and Pine Nuts in a Spicy Sauce

23. CRISPY BEEF*
With Tangerine Peels in Chef's Special Sauce

24. PLUM TREE SPECIAL
Lobster, Chicken, Roast Pork, Mushrooms, Bamboo Shoots, Water Chestnuts, Snow Peas with Special Sauce

√ = Recommended *** = Spicy**

▼

✓TO CHOOSE

Use these lists to order healthfully in your favorite Chinese restaurants.

Drinks (Yum Pun)

Chrysanthemum, jasmine, lichee teas, which assume the scent and flavor of fruits or flowers
Dragon well (the most famous of all green teas): grown in Chekiang province
Lo cha (semifermented or semigreen tea): light and delicate
Oolong (semigreen tea): fruity aroma, delicious after a Chinese dinner

***Choose* semigreen and scented Chinese teas that haven't been steeped a long time. Drink them in moderation and not too late in the day because they contain caffeine, but less than dark Chinese teas.**
***BEST BET:* Jasmine tea**

Appetizers (Dim Sum)

Beef *fun* roll
Cha shao dumplings
Chicken and glutinous rice wrapped in lotus leaves
Chicken bun
Dried shrimp *fun* roll
Paper-wrapped prawns
Shrimp *fun* roll
Shrimp *har gow*
Shrimp (prawn) dumplings
Steamed bean curd roll
Steamed shrimp *fun quo*
Stuffed bell pepper

✓ TO CHOOSE

Stuffed pancakes
Shao-mai (pork dumplings)

Choose **dumplings and *dim sum* that are paper-wrapped or steamed for breakfast.**
BEST BETS: **Shrimp (prawn) dumplings, *shao-mai* (pork dumplings)**

Soups (Tong)

Bird's nest soup
Chicken broth, green peas, and mushrooms
Chinese greens vegetable soup
Crab meat and asparagus soup: an American favorite
Egg drop soup: omit the egg yolk
Family watercress soup
Homemade chicken broth
Hot-and-sour soup: one serving contains 180 calories
Peking soup
Sam shin (noodles, chicken, seafood, and vegetables): a meal in itself
Shark fin soup: very expensive, delicious, and healthful
Shredded pork and noodle soup
Sliced pork and Szechuan vegetable soup
Wonton soup

Choose **soups with a clear broth and plenty of vegetables.**
BEST BETS: **Hot-and-sour soup or wonton soup**

Noodles (Mein), Rice (Fan), Porridge (Juk), and Dumplings (Gow)

Cold spicy noodles: refreshing on a hot day
Congee, also called *juk* (rice cooked with a lot of chicken

✓TO CHOOSE

broth or water and very small pieces of vegetables and meats): a nourishing meal for a tired stomach or anyone who is sick

Dumplings with sweet filling

Lotus bow (steamed buns that can be filled with meats and vegetables)

Noodles with meat sauce mixture: may have been the first "spaghetti"

Potstickers (steamed dumplings): delicious with hot chili sauce, rice vinegar, and grated ginger; request chicken

Soft noodles or *lo mein* with oyster sauce: go light on the oil and sauce

Stir-fried rice: request without ham and soy sauce

Subgum fried rice (chicken, peas, mushrooms, onions, and eggs are added to cooked rice that is quickly fried in a little oil): ask the chef to go light on the soy sauce

Wontons in broth (dumplings floating in broth): a delicious light lunch or dinner

Young jewel fried rice (most famous fried rice): go light on the soy sauce and oil

***Choose* rice, noodles, or dumplings—steamed or sautéed in very little oil—at every meal.**

***BEST BETS:* Lo mein (soft noodles with oyster sauce) or *subgum* fried rice**

Salads and Vegetables (Choy)

Asparagus with oyster sauce

Assorted vegetable dish: very popular

Broccoli with straw mushrooms

Buddha's delight (vegetarian plate): request your favorite vegetables steamed; this dish contains *tofu* (soy bean curd)

✓ TO CHOOSE

Celery hearts in mustard sauce
Chinese mixed green vegetables
Chop suey (vegetable *chop suey*): a pseudo-Chinese dish, but a delicious one
Chow mein (a pseudo-Chinese dish)
Cold Chinese salad
Mushrooms with string beans: delicious!
Mustard greens: delicious sautéed
Pea pods with black mushrooms
Pea shoots: very tender
Spicy steamed eggplant
Stir-fried broccoli in oyster sauce
Stir-fried Chinese cabbage
Two winters (combines black mushrooms and bamboo shoots, two vegetables at their best during the winter months)
Swamp shrimp: delicious with fermented bean curd
Szechuan preserved vegetable with bean curd (made with mustard greens, and hot spices)

***Choose* vegetables made without a lot of oil.**
***BEST BETS:* Buddha's delight, mushrooms with string beans, mustard greens, or pea pods with black mushrooms**

Beef (Nagu Yoke)

Barbecued beef
Beef and asparagus with black bean sauce
Beef *chop suey*
Beef *lo mein* with oyster sauce
Beef with bean curd
Beef with cauliflower
Beef with Chinese cabbage

✓To Choose

Beef with pea pods and water chestnuts
Ginger beef
Ground steak with peas
Mongolian barbecue: a meal that's as satisfying as a banquet
Sliced beef with broccoli
Sliced beef with curry sauce
Stewed beef in casserole
Stir-fried beef with green peppers: can be made without oil
Stir-fried beef with hot sauce: go light with the oil
Stir-fried beef with scallions

***Choose* beef dishes made without a lot of oil or soy sauce.**
***BEST BETS:* Stir-fried beef with green peppers, beef with pea pods and water chestnuts, or sliced beef with broccoli**

Pork (Gee Yoke)

Barbecued pork loin: this pork is lean
Bean sprouts with pork: lean pork is generally used
Diced pork with vegetables: lean pork is generally used
Lean pork with broccoli in oyster sauce (*ho yau gai laan*)
Pork cooked in barbecue sauce
Shredded pork in fish sauce
Shredded pork with squid

***Choose* lean pork dishes made without a lot of oil or soy sauce.**
***BEST BETS:* Diced pork with vegetables or bean sprouts with pork**

Chicken (Gai)

✓To Choose

Chicken *chow mein*: request very little oil
Chicken with chestnuts (a chestnut is a vegetable, not a nut)
Chili chicken cubes
Drunken chicken (marinated in wine, but the alcohol is cooked off)
Moo goo gai pan (sliced chicken with mushrooms): a very healthful dish
Paper-wrapped chicken
Red-cooked chicken
Shredded chicken with peppers
Steamed chicken with Chinese dried mushrooms
Steamed chicken with scallions
Stir-fried chicken with cashews: nuts are fattening; limit them
White meat chicken, pineapple, and Chinese vegetables

***Choose* chicken dishes made with skinless white meat and very little oil.**
***BEST BETS: Moo goo gai pan* or shredded chicken with peppers**

Duck (Opp) and Goose (Guil)

Avoid duck and goose because no matter what preparation method is used, they contain too much fat.

Fish (Yu)

Abalone with oyster sauce
Bean curd and shrimp
Chow mein with shrimp and pork: a popular pseudo-Chinese dish

✓To Choose

Crabmeat and eggs: Chinese people love seafood with eggs; discard one yolk
Lobster: lobster is called "dragon prawn" in Chinese; some have no claws, but the tail is bigger
Lobster Cantonese
Poached fish
Red-cooked yellow fish
Sautéed sliced prawns: very common dish
Smoked pomfret: hold the mayo
Stir-fried abalone with black mushrooms in oyster sauce
Stir-fried scallops with broccoli

***Choose* fish and shellfish dishes that have been steamed, poached, sautéed, or stir-fried.**
***BEST BETS:* Lobster Cantonese, poached fish, or sautéed sliced prawns**

Lamb (Yung)

Avoid lamb dishes, because no matter what the preparation method, lamb contains too much fat to be part of a healthful diet.

Egg Dishes (Tan)

Scrambled eggs with shark fin: expensive
Scrambled eggs with shrimp
Scrambled eggs with vegetable: bean sprouts are good
Sliced beef with scrambled eggs: ask the chef to throw away one yolk
Stir-fried shrimp with egg white: *fu jung* means "poached egg whites and shrimp or crabmeat"

✓ To Choose

Choose **egg dishes that are stir-fried.**
BEST BET: **Stir-fried shrimp with egg white**

Sauces (Tseung)

Black bean sauce: delicious on meats or with rice; may contain small amounts of sugar and salt
Hoi sin (seafood sauce): used for barbecues; some Americans call it duck sauce
Ho you (oyster sauce): made from real oysters and oyster extract
Lo she yau (dark soy sauce): contains less salt than light soy sauce and more molasses
Sun Tao (garlic sauce): usually not too much oil
Wong Wu (brown sauce): contains soy sauce, molasses, corn starch, and a little oil

Choose **less salty and sweet delicate thin sauces.**
BEST BET: **Black bean sauce, if diet permits sugar and salt**

Desserts (Tim Pun)

Apple: a token of harmony and peace
Canton orange: symbolizes happiness and prosperity
Fortune cookie: if the fortune is good, 65 calories each
Mi zhi zi (steamed pears in honey)
Peach: represents marriage and immortality
Plum: depicts winter and longevity

Choose **desserts that are made without sugar. (It's hard to get into trouble eating dessert in a Chinese restaurant, because most of the time, they aren't available.)**
BEST BET: **Fresh fruits**

⊘ TO AVOID

Drinks

Chinese beer: drink alcoholic beverages in moderation, diet permitting
Chinese rice wine: 4 ounces equals 152 calories; drink in moderation, diet permitting
Earl Grey (black China and Darjeeling tea blend)
Lapsang souchong (black China tea)

***Avoid* dark Chinese teas; they contain too much caffeine. Avoid drinking hard liquor.**

Appetizers

Chicken sticks
Chicken wings: too fatty
Crab puff (deep-fried)
Diamond shrimp balls (deep-fried)
Egg roll: fried and fattening—one equals 330 calories
Fried shrimp
Fried *wontons* (deep-fried and served with sweet-and-sour sauce)
Shrimp toast (fried)

***Avoid* appetizers that are deep-fried or made with a lot of oil.**

Soups

Chicken asparagus soup (usually a creamed soup)
Egg noodles in soup: order plain noodles instead and avoid the cholesterol
Fun see soup (ham and egg)
Sizzling rice soup (fried in oil)

⊘ TO AVOID

***Avoid* soups made with egg noodles or ham.**

Rice

Fried rice: contains a lot of soy sauce and oil
Fried rice with duck
Fried rice with pork: 1 cup equals 460 calories
Ham fried rice

***Avoid* rice that contains a lot of soy sauce or has been fried in a lot of oil**

Salads and Vegetables

Creamed Chinese cabbage: too much cream
Pickled sweet-and-sour vegetables: too salty
Sautéed spinach
Stir-fried sweet-and-sour cabbage
Tender-fried zucchini

***Avoid* creamed, salty, or fatty vegetables.**

Beef

Braised soy sauce beef
Crisp-fried shredded beef with vegetables: too oily
Sizzling beef
Szechuan shredded beef

***Avoid* fried beef dishes.**

Pork

Barbecued spareribs: too fatty
Braised pork with brown sauce: too much sugar and soy sauce

⊘TO AVOID

Braised spareribs with black bean sauce: too salty
Chinese pork sausage
Fried pork chops (*deen chi yuk*)
Moo shu pork (pork and mushrooms with egg wrapped inside a Chinese pancake): contains egg yolks and too much salt and oil; one serving equals more than 300 calories
Sautéed pork kidney: organ meats are loaded with cholesterol
Spareribs with garlic sauce (*dau she pai gwat*): seasoned with salted, cured soy beans, garlic, ginger, and soy sauce; 6 ounces equals 850 calories
Sweet-and-sour pork (*tim seun yuk*): contains oil and sugar
Twice-cooked pork: very popular, but too oily

***Avoid* fatty cuts of pork, particularly with the skin.**

Chicken

Chicken wings with oyster sauce: the skin is fatty
Chicken with cashews: nuts are full of fat; one serving equals 375 calories
Chicken with Chinese greens and ham: ham is fatty, salty, and contains nitrates
Chicken with walnuts: nuts are fatty, and this dish is deep-fried
Deep-fried battered chicken with black mushrooms and pea pods
Jade chicken: contains ham
Kung pao chicken (a popular deep-fried Szechuan dish)
Lemon chicken (coated and deep-fried)
Lychee chicken with sweet-and-sour sauce (deep-fried dish made with a lot of sugar)

⊘ TO AVOID

Soy chicken: too salty
Sweet-and-sour chicken

***Avoid* deep-fried chicken and chicken with sweet-and-sour sauce.**

Duck and Goose

Cantonese-style roasted duck
Crispy-skin duck
Peking duck: too fatty
Roasted goose: too fatty

***Avoid* duck and goose; they are too fatty.**

Fish

Baby and mother shrimps: contains too much sugar and ketchup
Cashew shrimp: nuts are mainly fat
Crispy-fried shrimp with garlic
Crispy squid: deep-fried; eaten like American onion rings
Deep-fried battered shrimp
Fried oyster rolls (dipped in batter and deep-fried)
Fried prawn with baby corn
Fried soft-shell crab
Sautéed prawns with tomato sauce: contains too much ketchup
Scallion-oil fillets: loaded with oil
Scallops in oyster sauce
Shrimp egg rolls (deep-fried)
Shrimp with peas (deep-fried)
Sweet-and-sour whole fish: too much sugar

⊘TO AVOID

Avoid **deep-fried fish and fish with sweet-and-sour sauce.**

Egg Dishes

Egg *fu yung* (fried)
Four happiness eggs: this fried dish represents prosperity, longevity, health, and happiness
Lui wang tsai (many dishes contain egg whites; this one contains egg yolks only)
Steamed custard

Avoid **egg dishes that are fried. If your cholesterol is high, avoid foods in shrimp or oyster sauce, egg drop soup, fried rice, and *moo shu* dishes because they contain little bits of scrambled egg yolk.**

Sauces

Sang she yau (light soy sauce): contains more salt than the dark variety; avoid them both if you're on a salt-restricted diet
So mooi tseung (plum sauce made of plums, spices, and quite a bit of sugar)
Tim mein tseung (sweet sauce served with Peking duck)

Avoid **thick sauces that contain a lot of cornstarch, salt, or sugar.**

Desserts

Eight precious rice pudding
Moon cakes: too much sugar and butter
Steamed bread pudding: contains eggs and butter
Steamed Chinese jelly roll

Avoid **desserts that contain sugar and butter.**

Chinese Defensive Dining Tips

When ordering Chinese food, here are some tips that will make your meals more delicious, authentic, and adaptable to your special eating requirements.

1. Order à la carte—made-to-order—Chinese dishes, rather than the suggested family-style dinners, which are not as fresh, since they've been made ahead of time and left in the steam table to stay warm.
2. Order *wonton* soup often because it must be made fresh. (Chicken, shrimp, black mushrooms, abalone, water chestnuts, pea pods, and bamboo shoots are added to the basic soup stock.)
3. Ask if there are any specials. Chinese waiters assume that non-Asian people have American tastes, so they don't mention them. If none of the specials sound appealing, request dishes that aren't on the menu, such as shark's fin soup (reputed to be an aphrodisiac), spicy bean curd or eggplant (good with steamed rice), steamed fish (find out what's fresh), black mushroom with bamboo shoots, or *lo mein* (soft noodles).
4. Do not order *the soup of the day* in a Chinese restaurant. Usually it has been made ahead of time and warmed in the steam table all day, rather than made fresh like most Chinese soups.
5. Eat with chopsticks, if you can. They make you eat slower, which gives you time to feel full and helps you eat less.
6. Ask to have the Chinese dishes you ordered cooked in water, chicken broth, or very little oil.

7. Avoid eating too much soy sauce; it is loaded with salt, which contributes to water retention and weight gain.
8. To take the place of soy sauce, order dishes seasoned with a dash of rice wine vinegar (*jiu*), ginger (*geung*), garlic (*sui tou*), chili oil (*lot yau*), and sherry.
9. Select Chinese dishes that are made with lots of vegetables and meat, chicken, or fish used as a condiment.
10. Ask to have the skin removed from Chinese chicken dishes before they are cooked.
11. Accompany your Chinese meal with plenty of steamed white rice rather than fried rice.
12. Tell the waiter to leave the MSG out of your food.
13. Use Menu Command, order less food, avoid soy sauce, and follow this old Chinese philosophy: "Leave the table only 70 percent full."

Chinese Phrases

In Chinese restaurants the food is usually made to order, so it's possible to have dishes customized to your specifications. Here are phrases to show the waiter so you can get what you want in any Chinese restaurant.

1. **Please bring me a dish of stir-fried Chinese vegetables cooked in chicken broth, instead of oil. Thanks.**
   Cheng pai gui yet dip gai tong chow choy ng-ho lok yul. Ng goi.

2. **Please bring me a mixture of stir-fried vegetables and lean beef, cooked in very little oil.**
   Cheng pai gui yet dip nau yoke chow choy lok sil-sil yul.

3. **Please bring me a mixture of stir-fried vegetables and chicken without the skin cooked in very little oil.**
   Cheng pai gui yet dip hui pei kai chow choy lok sil-sil yul.

4. **Please bring me a mixture of stir-fried vegetables and lean pork, cooked in very little oil.**
   Cheng pai gui yet dip shui cho yoke chow choy lok sil-sil yul.
5. **I'd like a side dish of plain white rice, too. Thanks.**
   Cheng pai gui yet dip pak, fan. Ng goi.
6. **Please do not add MSG to my food.**
   Cheng ng ho lok may ging.
7. **Please do not cook my food with soy sauce.**
   Cheng ng ho lok shi yul.
8. **All I need now is the check. Thanks.**
   Mai tan. Ng goi.

The Bottom Line

Although Chinese restaurants are not known for their decor or service, Chinese food is ranked high in taste and nutrition. In every Chinese restaurant you can order a big bowl of steamed white rice with stir-fried lean meats, tofu, and crisp and colorful vegetables for a mound of food that's as satisfying as a banquet. If you order a variety of foods, a Chinese meal can provide the correct proportions of carbohydrates (vegetables and rice) to protein (meats and tofu).

I like the way Madame Wong describes how to establish variety when it comes to choosing your meat courses in a Chinese restaurant. "A meal," she explains in her *Long-Life Chinese Cookbook*, "will be ideally balanced if a dish is selected from the animals that live in the land, sea, and air. Pork, beef, and lamb form the land force; the fowls make up the air force; and seafood belongs to the navy."

Avoid deep-fried dishes. Order, instead, food that has been prepared using one of the more healthful styles that complement a healthy diet. Although the Chinese diet is basically healthful, it eliminates dairy products. That, of course, is beneficial for people who are allergic to milk products, but for others it can lead to calcium deficiencies. Greens, broccoli, and tofu satisfy some of the needs we have for this mineral, but sometimes that is not enough. The Chinese diet can also be deficient in vitamin C, because not many fresh fruits are included.

So when eating Chinese food regularly, remember to supplement your diet with foods rich in calcium and vitamin C to obtain all the nutrients you need. In the next chapter, you'll see, similar health principles apply to everyone who enjoys Japanese.

Chin-Chin! (To your good health!)

Chapter 9

▲

JAPANESE FOOD

IN Japan, good living is synonymous with good eating. And the Japanese diet, which includes nutritionally sound fresh foods, plays an important role in the increased life expectancy of the Japanese people.

People from Japan now have a longer life expectancy than people from any other nation. Japanese men can expect to live to seventy-six years, which is five years longer than American men. The life expectancy of Japanese women is eighty-one years, which is three years longer than American women. Japanese people have cholesterol counts 20 percent, or more, below those typically found in the United States, and one of the world's lowest levels of heart disease.

It's not surprising that Japanese food has become more popular since there has been an increased interest in better health.

Japanese Regional Cooking

Generally speaking, the food is pretty much the same throughout Japan. People eat a lot of rice with pickled cabbage, cucumbers, or radishes and lots of fish for protein. Soy beans and soy bean products such as ***tofu*** (soy bean curd) and ***miso*** (soy bean paste) are other important sources of protein for the Japanese. To flavor their food, soy sauce (a salty brown sauce made from fermented soy beans) is widely used.

Restaurant Dining in Japan

There are more restaurants and more types of specialty restaurants in Japan per capita than anywhere else in the world because a restaurant meal is considered far more exciting to the Japanese than a homemade one. Japanese people like to dine in an uncluttered environment, so nothing distracts them from the full enjoyment of a meal, and most people's homes are too crowded to be serene.

Every restaurant in Japan is filled with people socializing for business or pleasure. The Japanese believe that no deal should be consummated without the parties first eating and drinking together. That, to them, is far more binding than a contract.

In most of the more formal restaurants you can request dishes from the menu, or say, "***Omakase***" ("Cook for me whatever you are in the mood to make"). This allows the chef to show off his talents and use the freshest fish and other ingredients that were selected at the market that day.

Kaiseki

If you'd rather have a preset menu, ***kaiseki*** (Japanese classical cuisine) may be the way to go. ***Kaiseki*** is served in some of the larger restaurants in Japan, where the foods are prepared in a particular way and served in a certain order with variety of flavors being the primary goal. As many as twelve courses may be presented so you won't get tired of any one taste. The dishes the chef creates are influenced by the climate, vegetables in season, the standards of the people, and the culture in each prefecture (state).

A *kaiseki* meal is usually a healthful one, because subtle, delicate sauces are used rather than those that are thick and coat the food. Although a *kaiseki* dinner costs between $80 and $235 per person, the experience is so memorable that it's worth the price. Ladies in kimonos present each item one by one like artwork, as *koto* music plays in the background. If you'd like to try a *kaiseki* meal, but don't want to spend a small fortune, the same experience is less expensive at lunchtime.

Specialty Restaurants

There are literally hundreds of little specialty restaurants throughout Japan's crowded, narrow streets, serving only one or two dishes such as *soba* (buckwheat noodles), *yakitori* (barbecued chicken), *teppan-yaki* (chicken or beef with vegetables cooked on a hot iron plate), or *robatayaki* (artistically cut food that is quickly grilled). These restaurants are named after the food they serve, with the addition of the word *ya*, which means "shop": for instance, soba-ya, yakitora-ya, and so on. But even if you don't speak the language, it's easy to identify the type of food being served, because plastic models of the food are displayed in the windows of some restaurants. Prices are also indicated.

Kissaten

Kissaten are small coffee shops that resemble the American coffee shop. They are particularly plentiful in the urban areas, providing casual meeting places for people to talk, listen to music, drink coffee or black tea, and have a bite to eat. Fresh fruits, custards, Japanese sweets, and bean paste sundaes are usually available. *Kissaten* get busier after three o' clock in the afternoon, because in Japan baked goods are usually eaten as snacks rather than desserts.

Sushi Bars

Sushi (cold cooked rice flavored with vinegar and rolled in seaweed around raw fish and vegetables) is sold in full-menu Japanese restaurants and in *sushi* bars, which are on every major street. In addition, *sashimi* (thin slices of raw fish), *tempura* (fish and vegetables fried in batter), and other popular Japanese dishes are served. In *sushi* bars prices usually aren't marked on menus, so unless you want a big surprise when the bill arrives, ask how much items cost.

Shojin Ryori

For people on vegetarian diets, there are special restaurants in Japan called *shojin ryori*, which means "cooking only with vegetables." Sometimes *shojin ryori* is more expensive than other Japanese dishes because the chefs must think and work hard to bring out the natural flavor of foods without using meat and rich sauces.

Biya Gaadens

In addition to the many restaurants in Japan, there are "biya gaadens" (beer gardens) where people can meet and eat. The Japanese are master beer makers, and beer is a popular summertime beverage. *Sake* is preferred during the winter months, but if you're watching your weight, remember, all alcoholic beverages are high in calories and low in nutrients; one serving of *sake*, which fills approximately four little *sake* cups, equals 160 calories. And one bottle, or 12 fluid ounces, of Japanese beer contains 128 calories. (Remember, drink alcoholic beverages in moderation.)

O' Bento

People who don't want to eat in beer gardens or restaurants, yet still want something quickly, can purchase *o' bento* (lunch box) meals. *O' bento* foods come in neat compartmentalized boxes that can be bought daily throughout Japan. In the early mornings, housewives often prepare these lunches for their children. Grocery store proprietors and shop owners offer *o' bento* lunches to their customers. A typical *o' bento* lunch consists of a few pieces of deep-fried chicken or pork, *kamaboko* (slices of fish sausages), *nimono* (cooked vegetables), and pickles.

Japanese-American Restaurants

Sushi, sashimi, sukiyaki, yakiniku, and other delicious, healthful Japanese dishes make it possible to feast royally in Japanese restaurants in America. Main dishes are usually preceded by *miso* soup and salad—with a wine vinegar, honey, and sesame seed oil dressing—but if you need to avoid salt, I suggest you skip the *miso* soup and request extra salad or rice instead.

Americans generally end their Japanese dinners with ice cream, but I suggest fresh fruit instead when it's available; it's more refreshing, and Japanese people only serve fresh fruit that's sweet and juicy.

The Art of the Japanese Meal

The presentation of a meal is very important to Japanese people. Great care is taken to arrange food attractively in lacquer-coated or porcelain dishes, which are chosen to complement the foods' shape, color, and texture.

In the dining rooms of traditional Japanese restaurants, you will see customers sitting around low tables on cushions placed on the *tatami* (straw mat floor), eating their meals with pointed wooden chopsticks that have hand-painted pictures at the top. They eat first with their eyes, so the size, color, shape, arrangement of the food, and the plate it is presented on are important. And since many dishes are served at the same time, there is no such thing as the main course. That way, a different taste can be enjoyed with each bite.

Before eating a Japanese meal, it is polite to say, "*Itadakimasu*," which means "I'm going to dig in now." After finishing a Japanese meal, it's good manners to say, "*Gochisosama deshita*," which means, "I've feasted royally."

Low-Fat, Low-Calorie Foods

Most Japanese dishes are oil-free, and when recipes call for it, only moderate amounts of corn oil, a polyunsaturated fat, are added. Other ingredients are healthful too. Various types of seaweeds are often used in Japanese dishes. They are low in calories and an excellent source of dietary minerals.

Hjiki is cooked with soy sauce, sugar, and stock.
Kombu (another seaweed), *katsuo bushi* (dried bonito flakes), and water are used to make *dashi*, the stock in most Japanese recipes.
Nori is used to wrap *sushi* and garnish food.
Wakame is tossed in salads.

In addition to using several varieties of seaweed and other healthful ingredients, Japanese people use gentle cooking methods, so most of the vitamins and minerals in their food are left intact. These are their names and descriptions:

Itamemono—Stir-frying
Yakimono—Braising, grilling, and broiling
Kushiyaki—Grilled on a stick
Mushimono—Steaming
Nimono—Simmering

For a delicious Japanese breakfast, try fish, *tofu* (soy bean curd), egg—sometimes left over from the previous day—*miso* soup, tea, some seaweed, a tiny salty-sour plum, pickles, and rice. At lunch or dinner try a delicious dish called *sukiyaki* (thin slices of beef or chicken simmered with nappa cabbage, onions, bamboo shoots, mushrooms, and *shirataki*—transparent noodles). The broth is flavored with just a little soy sauce, *sake*, and sugar. It's nutritious because the water-soluble nutrients that leach out into the broth from cooking the meat and vegetables are part of the meal.

Fried Foods

All Japanese dishes are not healthful, however. *Agemano* (deep-fried) Japanese dishes such as *tempura* (shrimp, whitefish, and vegetables coated with batter and then deep-fried) should be avoided. Although the batter is usually light, it is fatty. *Tempura*, in fact, is one of the most caloric and least healthful dishes on the menu.

Salt

Salt is another problem with the Japanese diet. Although there is 6½ times more sodium in regular table salt than in soy sauce, the Japanese use soy sauce so liberally, they have a higher salt intake than any other people in the world, particularly in the bustling business district of Kanto (near Tokyo). People who live there tend to add soy sauce to their food, if it looks too light, before tasting it.

People who live in the Kansai (Osaka) area, where textile and steel businesses are thriving, appreciate the more natural tastes of food. They use less soy sauce then people from the more rural area of Japan and think it is rude for a person to use salt or soy sauce before tasting their food. To them, less salt doesn't necessarily mean less taste.

But no matter what area of Japan you're in, if you're concerned about high blood pressure or gaining weight due to water retention, avoid *miso* (fermented soy bean paste), *tsukemono* (pickled vegetables), and *shoyu* (soy sauce), because they're loaded with sodium.

Tiny dried fish are another salty addition to the Japanese diet. They are eaten to provide calcium, because Japanese people do not drink much milk or eat many dairy products. The fish taste good alone or with other foods, but people on a salt-restricted diet should avoid them. Decreased salt intake, coupled with weight maintenance and reduced alcohol consumption, could lessen your chances of developing high blood pressure in the future.

To further reduce the amount of salt in your diet when eating out, order food made without soy or other sauces or request "lite" soy sauce—which contains less salt—and then water it down with lemon juice before using it.

SUGAR

After fat, you may think that sugar is your main concern if you want to lose weight. But one teaspoon of sugar is usually all that's needed to balance out the salty taste in Japanese dishes that serve four to six. So sugar really isn't a problem, except for people with diabetes or hypoglycemia who should eliminate it from their diets completely.

People who must totally avoid simple sugar need to request their *teriyaki* (grilled beef, chicken, or fish seasoned with soy sauce, sugar, *sake*, and ginger) without sauce so they'll end up with a delicious piece of plain beef, chicken, or fish. If your diet allows a little sugar and salt, you may order *teriyaki* dishes if the waiter says the chef made the sauce mild and not too thick.

SUSHI AND SASHIMI

Sushi (vinegared rice with raw or cooked fish) and *sashimi* (fresh raw fish cut into thin slices) are two Japanese dishes many people get hooked on. They are nearly perfect foods, and there are no other dishes like them anywhere in the world.

Sushi and *sashimi* originated in Japan about a thousand years ago, and they were exclusively Japanese until they became chic in American-Japanese restaurants in recent years. *Sushi* and *sashimi* are served alone or any time during a meal, in three different ways: *nigirizushi*, *makizushi*, and *chirashizushi*.

Nigirizushi is a long mound of vinegared rice topped with a longer piece of raw fish.

Makizushi is vinegared rice and raw fish or vegetables rolled in sheets of seaweed and then cut into pieces.

Chirashizushi is assorted raw and cooked fish on loose vinegared rice.

What an adventure it is sitting down at a *sushi* bar and watching the *itamae* (*sushi* man) skillfully prepare delicacies that look like works of art you pop into your mouth. The way the *sushi* man's hands work so quickly looks like magic. Shredded *daikon* (Japanese white radish) usually accompanies the dishes the *itamae* makes.

A small dab of *wasabi* (a strong, green horseradish paste) is generally brushed on the *sushi* between the rice and the fish to add flavor. *Wasabi* is also served on the side. I recommend you drink a lot of water when you use it and only eat a moderate amount because it is very strong. *Shoga* (sweet pickled ginger) and *shoyu* (soy sauce) also accompany *sushi* and *sashimi*. Beware of these condiments if you are avoiding salt.

Many people are concerned about the *kiseichu* (parasites) they have heard may be in *sushi*. Parasites in *sushi* are not prevalent today, because most *sushi* bars are clean and serve fresh fish that has been candled—held up to the light to see if larvae are present. I've seen people in *sushi* bars with flashlights candling fish themselves, looking for an opaque area that might prove to be a coiled worm.

The types of fish that most often contain larvae are *sake* (salmon) and *hamachi* (yellowtail). Freezing kills parasites, however, so as a precaution eat salmon or yellowtail only if it has been frozen and then cooked. The Japanese Menu Command in this chapter contains a complete list of *sushi* and *sashimi* to avoid and enjoy.

Japanese Fast Food

For centuries you couldn't buy fast food in Japan except for a ham-and-cheese, chicken, or beef sandwich at a *sandoitchi* shop. As people got busier, left their homes, and entered the work force, something was needed and American fast food became popular in Japan. Now, next to the sandwich shops you can find McDonald's, and other fast food spots.

Japanese-American Fast Foods

Sushi was first made in Japan. The Japanese consider *sushi* a delicacy that must be made fresh. It's a food to eat when you can sit down, take your time, and enjoy yourself. So, premade *sushi* available in most larger American cities is not typically eaten by the Japanese.

Spaghetti Houses

When Japanese people don't have time to spare, yet want some food that's filling, they often drop by a spaghetti house for a quick bite to eat.

If you stop into one of these restaurants, you may have a hard time deciding what to order, because many things on the menu look good. Try dishes like spaghetti with curry sauce (spaghetti with curry sauce, shredded beef, mushrooms, bell peppers, and mushrooms), or vegetable spaghetti Japanese style (spaghetti with tomatoes, green beans, mushrooms, bell peppers, and onions flavored with soy sauce). They're delicious, and priced right, too!

Although the food is totally different from anything you've ever tasted in an Italian spaghetti house, once you've tried it, you'll probably want to go again. With drinks, two people can eat for about $11. It's possible to eat relatively inexpensively at other typically Japanese restaurants, too.

▲

Noma Menu

The dishes checked off on this menu from Noma, located in West Los Angeles, are nutritious, low-fat, low-salt, high-fiber choices you can include in your healthful eating plan.

Dinner

(SALAD, SOUP, RICE AND DESSERT)

FISH TEMPURA White Meat Fish and Fresh Vegetable

COMBINATION TEMPURA Shrimp and Fresh Vegetable Prepared in a Delicate Batter

SEAFOOD TEMPURA Shrimp, White Meat Fish, Scallop and Vegetable

√ TERIYAKI (Beef or Chicken) Broiled Steak Seasoned with Teriyaki Sauce [NOTE: Order if your diet permits a touch of sugar and salt]

√ YAKITORI (Chicken) Japanese Shish Kabob with Vegetables Seasoned with Teriyaki Sauce [NOTE: Order if your diet permits a touch of sugar and salt]

√ SUKIYAKI (Beef or Chicken) A Traditional Japanese Meat and Vegetable Dish

√ = Recommended

BEEF BUTTERYAKI Sliced Tender Beef, Mushrooms, Broccoli and Bamboo Shoots

√ GINGER BEEF Sliced Beef, Broccoli, Mushrooms and Bamboo Shoots

CALIFORNIA CHICKEN TEMPURA Chicken Breast, Stuffed Avocado, Prepared in a Delicate Batter

CHICKEN CUTLET

Seafood Dinner

(SALAD, SOUP, RICE AND DESSERT)

√ SAUTEED ORANGE ROUGHY

√ BAKED ORANGE ROUGHY

√ SASHIMI DINNER Mixed Raw Fish (Tuna, Whitefish, Yellowtail, Giant Clam, Mackerel)

√ SALMON TERIYAKI Alaskan King Salmon, Teriyaki Sauce

SCALLOP and SHRIMP BUTTERYAKI Scallop, Shrimp, Mushrooms, Bamboo Shoots, Broccoli and Garlic

√ GRILLED YELLOWTAIL With Teriyaki or Ponzu Sauce

√ BROCHETTE OF SEAFOOD With Ginger Sauce, Shrimps, Scallop and Salmon with Vegetable

√ SAUTEED MAHIMAHI STEAK

Dessert

GREEN TEA ICE CREAM

GINGER ICE CREAM

√ FRESH FRUIT

Beverage

GENSHU SAKE

PLUM WINE

SAKE

SAPPORO and KIRIN DRAFT

BEER: Kirin, Michelob

LIGHT BEER: Kirin, Michelob

CALIFORNIA WINE

7-UP, COKE

√ = **Recommended**

√ PERRIER
DIET SODA
√ MILK (nonfat)
√ ORANGE JUICE

Yakiniku Dinner
(SALAD, SOUP, RICE AND DESSERT)
√ CHICKEN YAKINIKU Slices of Chicken and Fresh Vegetable Seasoned with Our Own Sauce
√ BEEF YAKINIKU Slices of Tender Beef and Fresh Vegetable Seasoned with Our Own Yakiniku Sauce
LAMB YAKINIKU Slices of Leg of Lamb and Fresh Vegetable Seasoned with Our Own Sauce
NOMA'S COMBINATION YAKINIKU Your Choice of Meat (Beef, Chicken or Lamb) and Shrimp, Scallop and Fresh Vegetable

Vegetarian Corner
VEGETABLE TEMPURA
√ VEGETABLE SUKIYAKI
√ FRESH VEGETABLE

Combination Dinner
(SALAD, SOUP, RICE AND DESSERT)
1. TEMPURA and YAKINIKU
2. TEMPURA and SUKIYAKI
3. TEMPURA and SASHIMI
4. TEMPURA and SUSHI
5. TEMPURA and TERIYAKI
6. TEMPURA and YAKITORI
√ 7. YAKINIKU and SASHIMI
√ 8. YAKINIKU and SUSHI
9. TEMPURA, SHRIMP and SCALLOP BUTTERYAKI
10. SASHIMI, TEMPURA and YAKINIKU
11. SASHIMI, TEMPURA and CHICKEN or BEEF TERIYAKI
12. SASHIMI, TEMPURA and CHICKEN CUTLET

▼

√ = **Recommended**

✓TO CHOOSE

Use this Japanese Menu Command, so you'll know which dishes to order in every category.

Drinks (Nomimono)

Bancha (Japanese green tea, low in caffeine)
Genmaicha (low in caffeine)
Gyokuro (expensive)
Matcha (expensive, ceremonial green tea)
Mineral water

Choose weak teas that are low in caffeine.
***BEST BETS:* Bancha and Genmaicha; they have less caffeine**

Appetizers (Zensai)

Japanese-style steamed clam
Kushiyaki (chicken or beef on a stick)
Natto-tofu (fermented soy beans and soy bean curd)
Sashimi (sliced raw fish)
Soft-shell crab
Steamed green mussel
Sushi (sliced raw fish with vinegared rice)
Yakitori (grilled chicken)

***Choose* appetizers that aren't fried or topped with salty and sugary sauces.**

BEST BETS: sushi, sashimi,* and *yakitori

One-Pot (Nabemono) Dishes

Japanese-style *bouillabaisse* (shrimp, salmon, whitefish, green mussel, clam, and vegetable)

✓TO CHOOSE

Mizutaki (small pieces of chicken, lean pork, tofu, nappa cabbage, carrots, bean sprouts, *shirataki*, bamboo shoots, watercress, and Japanese mushrooms): have the chicken skinned before cooking
Oden (various kinds of fish cakes cooked in stock with *konnyaku*—yam cake—and *daikon*—white radish)
Shabu shabu (thinly sliced meat and vegetables cooked in a bubbling broth): each bite is dipped in sauce
Sukiyaki (thin slices of lean beef or chicken simmered with assorted vegetables in a delicate broth)
Uosuki (*sukiyaki* made with fish instead of beef or chicken)

***Choose* one-pot dishes often; they're loaded with nutrients.**
BEST BETS: Sukiyaki, shabu shabu, uosuki

Bean Curd (Tofu) Dishes

Dengaku (grilled tofu with *miso*)
Hiyayakko (uncooked, chilled tofu served with chopped green onion, bonito flake, and soy sauce)
Iridofu (tofu scrambled with chicken and peas)
Mabodofu (lean ground beef and tofu cooked with ingredients similar to those used in spaghetti sauce)
Yudofu (cooked, hot tofu): when you eat it, dip it in stock

***Choose* tofu often; it contains lots of calcium.**
BEST BETS: Hiyayakko, yudofu, dengaku

Japanese-Style Noodles (Menrui)

SOBA (handmade Japanese buckwheat noodles):
Cha-Soba (cold green tea–flavored noodles)

✓To Choose

Nishinsoba (*soba* with cooked herring)
Wakamesoba (seaweed *soba*)
Zarusoba (cold noodles served separately)

SOMEN (thin wheat noodles):
Hiyashisomen (cold)
Nyumen (hot)

UDON (thick round wheat noodles):
Curry *Udon* (noodles with curry)
Nabeyakiudon (green onion, *kamaboko*, egg, bamboo shoots, and shrimp *tempura*)
Nikuudon (thick round noodles with beef)

***Choose* noodle dishes often; they are delicious and high in complex carbohydrates, so they provide a lot of energy.**
***BEST BETS: Nishinsoba,* if your diet allows salt**

Soups (Suimono)

Miso (broth thickened with fermented bean paste)
Sumashijiru (clear soup)

***Choose* Japanese soups, if you can afford the salt.**
***BEST BET: Miso* soup**

Rice Dishes (Gohan)

Chameshi (tea rice—*dashi* and tea poured over rice)
Chazuke (rice with tea)
Kamameshi (pot rice—a variety of seafood, meats, and vegetables, chopped and cooked with rice)
Zosui (special-flavored rice porridge)

✓To Choose

Choose **rice dishes made with lean meat, fish, and vegetables.**
BEST BETS: Kamameshi, zosui

Sushi and Sashimi

NIGIRIZUSHI (mound of vinegared rice topped with a piece of raw fish):
Aji (Spanish mackerel)
Amaebi (sweet shrimp)
Anago (sea eel)
Awabi (abalone)
Ebi (shrimp)
Hamachi (yellowtail): if it was frozen first
Hirame (halibut)
Kaibashira (scallop)
Kaki (oyster)
Katsuo (bonito)
Maguro (dark meat tuna)
Masago (smelt egg)
Saba (mackerel)
Sake (salmon): if it was frozen first
Tako (octopus)
Tamago (egg)
Tobiko (flying fish egg)
Toro (white meat tuna belly)

MAKIZUSHI (vinegared *sushi* rice and raw fish or vegetables rolled in sheets of seaweed and cut into pieces):
Anakyu (sea eel and cucumber roll)
California roll (avocado roll): contains very little avocado

✓To Choose

Kappamaki (cucumber roll)
Salmon skin (salmon skin roll)
Shinkomaki (pickled white radish roll)
Tekka (tuna roll)
Vegetable (vegetable roll)

CHIRASHIZUSHI (loose vinegared *sushi* rice covered with a variety of fish)

***Choose sushi* and *sashimi* often; they are delicious.**
BEST BETS: Amaebi, hirame, maguro, and tekka

Dressed Salads (Sunomono)

Cucumber and crab salad (with Japanese vinegar dressing)
Cucumber and shrimp salad (with Japanese vinegar dressing)
Cucumber, avocado, and crab salad (with Japanese vinegar dressing)
Kani-Su (crabmeat salad)
Wakame-Su (seaweed and cucumber salad)

Vegetables (Nimomo)

Bamboo shoots simmered in amber sauce
Braised burdock root and carrot
Braised celery strips
Braised sea vegetable
Daikon (flat white radishes)
Enokidaké (slender creamy white mushrooms)
Japanese eggplant
Shiitake mushrooms (dark oak mushrooms when fresh, dark Oriental mushrooms when dried)
Shimeji mushrooms
Yasai (braised assorted vegetables)

JAPANESE FOOD

✓To Choose

Choose salads and vegetables that aren't too salty or sweet.
BEST BETS: Japanese eggplant, _shiitake_ mushrooms

Beef (Gyuniku)

Beef *kushiyaki* (skewered beef)
Beef *teriyaki* (broiled sliced beef with a soy-seasoned glaze): order if your diet allows some sugar and salt
Beef *yakiniku* (broiled or barbecued beef)
Ginger beef
Nikujaga (potatoes, carrots, and sliced beef in a natural gravy)
Sukiyaki (braised beef and vegetable dish)

Choose lean beef dishes that are braised or grilled.
BEST BETS: beef _yakiniku,_ beef _kushiyaki_

Chicken (Toriniku)

Chicken *teriyaki*: make sure the sauce isn't too sweet
Chicken *yakitori* (chicken broiled on a stick): make sure the sauce isn't too sweet
Chikuzenni (cooked chicken with Japanese vegetables; yam cake, burdock root, carrot, lotus root, and green peas are usually included)

Choose skinless chicken dishes without thick sauces.
BEST BETS: Chicken _yakitori, chikuzenni_

Fish (Sakana)

Awabi (abalone cooked with Japanese *sake* and served with mustard sauce)

✓TO CHOOSE

Black cod *teriyaki*
Brochette of seafood
Fugu (globefish): an expensive dish available only in Japan's finer restaurants
Lobster
Miso-marinated fish grill
Salmon *teriyaki*
Sautéed *mahimahi* steak
Sautéed orange roughy
Yellowtail grilled with *teriyaki* or *ponzu* sauce
Yosenabe (steamed seafoods and vegetables)

***Choose* Japanese fish dishes often; they are fresh and delicious**
***BEST BETS:* Black cod *teriyaki,* yellowtail grilled with *ponzu* sauce**

Sauces

Ponzu (Japanese vinegar, soy sauce, and citrus-juice dressing): this sauce is delicious!
Sujoyu (Japanese vinegar and soy sauce)
Teriyaki (sweet rice wine, soy sauce, *sake*, beef stock, salt and pepper, cornstarch)
Yakiniku (soy sauce, beef stock, sugar, Japanese sweet wine, Japanese wine, salt and pepper, garlic, ginger, onion, celery, carrot, bay leaf, thyme, and lemon)

***Choose* Japanese sauces if your diet permits a little salt and sugar.**
BEST BET: Ponzu* sauce, *sujoyu

Desserts (Dezato)

Fresh seasonal fruits

⊘TO AVOID

Drinks

Beer (Asahi, Kirin, Sapporo, Suntory)
Plum wine (sweet)
Sake (Japanese rice wine): usually heated to 108 degrees

Avoid **all types of hard liquor, (large amounts of) caffeinated teas, and sugary drinks.**

Appetizers

Gyoza (fried dumplings)
Kani-agemano (fried crab)
Tempura (shrimps, whitefish and vegetables fried in batter)

Avoid **fried appetizers**

Tofu Dishes

Agedashidofu (fried tofu)

Avoid **tofu dishes that are fried.**

Rice

Fried rice
Fried rice wrapped with eggs
Katsudon (egg and pork cutlet over rice)
Oyakodonburi (egg and chicken over rice)
Tendon (*tempura* over rice)

Avoid **rice dishes with fried items.**

Sushi and Sashimi

Ika (squid)
Ikura (salmon roe)

⊘ To Avoid

Uni (sea urchin egg)
Unagi (river eel)

Avoid these items; they are high in cholesterol.

Noodles

Ikura oroshi soba (noodles topped with salmon egg and grated radish): high in cholesterol
Kitsune udon (thick round noodles with a piece of deep-fried bean curd)
Nabeyaki (noodles topped with *tempura*)
Tempura-soba (noodles served topped with a fried prawn)

***Avoid* noodle dishes topped with fried items.**

Salads and Vegetables

Deep-fried asparagus rolled in sea eel, served with deep-fried vegetable
Duck salad with assorted greens
Salmon skin salad (baked salmon skin, radish sprouts, and cucumber)
Seafood salad (crab, scallop, shrimp, clam, and octopus): contains mayonnaise
Vegetable *tempura*
Vegetarian patties: they are fried

***Avoid* mayonnaise-based dressings, fried vegetables, and Japanese salad dressing if you must restrict your intake of salt and sugar.**

Beef

Beef stew: the meat is usually fatty
New York steak *teriyaki*: too fatty

⊘ To Avoid

Avoid the more expensive cuts of beef; they are usually fattier than the less expensive ones.

Pork

Tonkatsu (pork cutlet)
Yakibuta (barbecued pork)

***Avoid* fried pork dishes and sweet sauces.**

Chicken

Chicken cutlet (breaded deep-fried chicken)
Chicken *tempura* (deep-fried chicken)
Chicken wrapped in bacon

***Avoid* fried chicken; especially the skin.**

Fish

Butter-fried lobster
Deep-fried catfish served whole
Deep-fried sole
Fish *tempura*
Fried oyster
Mashed shrimp and salmon meat wrapped with *gyoza* skin (deep-fried rolls served with a mustard vinegar)
Seafood *tempura*
Shrimp *tempura*
Unagi kabayaki (broiled eel served on top of rice): high in cholesterol
Yellowtail *shioyaki* (salt-broiled fish): too salty

***Avoid* fish that has been deep-fried.**

Egg Dishes

⊘TO AVOID

Chawanmushi (steamed egg custard in individual bowls, with diced green beans, white meat chicken, and shrimp)
Tamago dashimaki (flaky rolled omelet)

***Avoid* premade egg dishes, because you can't omit the yolks, which are high in cholesterol.**

Sauces

Japanese recipes call for great amounts of *sato* (sugar) in glazes and sauces to balance out the tartness of vinegar and the saltiness of the soy sauce that is used. You can use moderate amounts of Japanese sauces if your diet permits a little salt and sugar.

***Avoid* the mayonnaise-based dressings, however.**

Desserts

Ginger ice cream
Green tea ice cream
Pudin (pudding)
Tempura ice cream (fried ice cream)

***Avoid* fatty, sugary desserts.**

JAPANESE DEFENSIVE DINING TIPS

Here are nine tips to help you eat nutritiously while dining out in Japanese restaurants:

1. Learn to appreciate the nutritionally sound and simple foods in the Japanese diet.

2. Request food made without salt and soy sauce.
3. Avoid *miso* and pickled foods to cut down on the amount of salt in your diet.
4. Water down a little soy sauce and add lemon juice, right at your table, to use if your food tastes bland.
5. Request extra condiments such as *wasabi* (green horseradish) so you can add extra zip to your meal without added salt.
6. Supplement your diet with nonfat and low-fat dairy products, because they provide calcium and other nutrients you need.
7. Avoid deep-fried Japanese entrées including *tempura*-style batter-coated vegetables.
8. Eliminate ice cream and gooey desserts from your diet.
9. Drink *sake* and other alcoholic beverages in moderation.

JAPANESE PHRASES

In Japan you can point to the plastic models in restaurant windows to order food. However, if you want to make special requests, here are a few phrases you can use:

1. **Please bring me a Japanese salad with the dressing on the side. Thanks.**
   Sarada to dressing o betsu betsu ni kudasai.

2. **I'd like a combination *sushi* plate, made with the freshest fish available, but please, no salmon or yellowtail.**
   Sake to hamachi igai no osushi no moriawase o kudasai.

3. **Please cook my food without soy sauce.**
   Shoyu o tsukawanaide tsukutte kudasai.

4. **I'd like you to make my food without using sugar.**
   Osato o tsukawanaide tsukutte kudasai.

5. **Please bring me a piece of grilled salmon, with *teriyaki* sauce on the side. Thanks.**
   Sake o yaite, teriyaki soosu o betsu ni kudasai.

6. **I'd like a piece of grilled skinless chicken breast and some steamed white rice, thanks.**
   Kawa o totta toriniku o yaite, gohan to isshoni kudasai.

7. **I'd like a side dish of seasonal Japanese vegetables steamed or stir-fried.**
   Kisetsuno yasai no itamemono ka yugakimono o betsu ni kudasai.

8. **I'd like a side of steamed white rice.**
   Gohan mo betsuni kudasai.

9. **Please bring me a pot of green tea.**
   Ocha o kudasai.

10. **I'd like some fresh fruit to end the meal.**
    Saigoni shinsenna kudamono o kudasai.

The Bottom Line

Since Japanese dining offers small portions of basically healthful foods, it's easy to tailor the Japanese diet to your special needs. There are some problems indigenous to this cuisine, however. Since Japanese people don't drink a lot of milk or eat many dairy products, they may be lacking calcium. Tofu and dried fish contain calcium, and are often eaten instead, but along with other salty Japanese items they pose a problem to people who should be on low-salt diets. As patrons become more aware of their health needs, Japanese chefs are more willing to modify recipes.

So, now that you know which Japanese dishes to order and how to have them prepared, you'll be able to enjoy yourself more than ever in Japanese restaurants. With know-how, it's possible to avoid salty foods and incorporate calcium into your diet while enjoying Japanese dishes. You'll be able to add Indian foods to your eating plan, too, once you read the next chapter and find out what to do.

Doozo meshiagatte kudasai! (Enjoy yourselves!)

Chapter 10

▲

INDIAN FOOD

THERE is no one India or Indian cuisine. The country of India is a million and a half square miles of changing topography. There are more than seven hundred million people of various faiths, who speak fifteen official languages and hundreds of dialects. Those who can afford it, eat in restaurants often.

Ingredients such as rice, wheat, millet, and *pulses* (beans, chickpeas, and lentils pureed together) are included on most menus. No other cuisine combines beans and grains so beautifully. Although these healthful ingredients will keep your body strong, there are problems I'd like you to be on the lookout for when ordering this cuisine.

Indian chefs like to cook with *ghee* (clarified butter), an artery-clogging saturated fat. And the waiters, in an attempt to be hospitable, like to serve a variety of foods and coax their guests to overeat.

When your order is served, the waiters generally serve huge first portions. Then they replenish the food on your plate as fast as you've eaten. They think you haven't enjoyed yourself unless you've eaten three or four helpings, so it's common to leave an Indian restaurant feeling uncomfortably full.

Indian Regional Cooking

Climate, geography, and religion influence this cuisine, which varies not only from region to region, but also depending upon whether you are in northern or southern India.

Some Indians in the north are Moslems and meat eaters. They are cautious about eating pork and shellfish, however, because pigs feed on scraps that may be unclean, and they consider shellfish the scavengers of the sea. Moslems depend primarily on lamb for their diet. In India lamb is commonly known as mutton, but since it's fattier than fish or chicken, you'd be wise not to order it.

A typical Indian meal in northern India may include whole-wheat *chapatis* (thin, flat, baked breads that resemble tortillas), *basmati rice* (India's primary grain), *dal* (a porridge made of *pulses*), *chutney* (relish made of fruits, vegetables, and herbs), meat and vegetables in *curry* (herbs made into a special sauce), *raita* (a mixture of yogurt with fruits and vegetables), dessert made from milk, yogurt, fruits, and nuts, and a mango *lassi* (blended yogurt and mango drink)—delicious!

In contrast to the Moslems, the Hindus are vegetarians and do not eat meat because it is considered sacrilegious. Instead of meats, a vegetarian meal might include two or three vegetable dishes in addition to the other dishes I mentioned. But don't get fooled into thinking the Hindus are healthier than the Moslems. Vegetarian food in India can be so rich, fatty, and sugary, the people eating it become overweight. So please, avoid vegetarian food that is loaded with butter, cream, cheese, or sugar.

The Art of the Indian Meal

Although food throughout India varies, the customs are similar. When you walk into an Indian restaurant you should always wash your hands before the meal. Then, if it is offered, drink some water, but only purified or bottled water. After the water an appetizer may be presented, but the rest of a traditional Indian meal is not served or eaten in separate courses.

Each person eats the remainder of the meal from a plate that's divided into four compartments, or in small bowls arranged on a *thali* (a large metallic tray). Once food is placed in your *thali* or plate, it becomes *jutha* (inappropriate to offer to others unless that person is an immediate member of your family).

Indian people eat only with their right hand even if they are left-handed because the left hand, used to clean themselves after using the toilet, is considered unclean. Your left hand may be used, however, to break pieces of bread, scoop up accompanying dishes, or pick up your drink.

Tea and fruits, or very sweet desserts, are served at the end of an Indian meal. Water is brought around, after dinner, for you to wash your hands, and *paan* (a digestive preparation) is offered to chew on after the meal.

Indian tea (*chai*) comes in several varieties:

Ordinary Indian tea is made with loose tea, rather than tea bags, and is steeped for a short time.

Special teas are brewed in half milk and half water; they are brewed longer, so they are stronger than ordinary tea.

Pani kum is extra-special tea made from expensive imported tea leaves. It is made with more milk than water, and you are only served half a cup, because of its cost.

Masala tea is made with spices.

Istanbuli tea is made without milk; it is served in a special type of cup with a slice of lime, and sugar is added.

BREAD

Chapatis are only one of the many leavened and unleavened wheat, white, and millet breads available in India. Vegetarians and meat eaters alike depend upon several delicious varieties as their staff of life. Bread is used as an edible scooper for *curry* and other dishes when eating in the traditional style, with the fingers.

None of these breads keep well, however, so in most Indian restaurants they are made fresh daily.

Chapati (griddle-cooked, unleavened whole-wheat flat bread) is the most common type. I suggest you order this type but make sure it is not topped with butter.

Naan (leavened, thicker, white flat bread), made without oil, is usually baked in the *tandoor* oven on a plate. (A good choice.)

Puris (fried, unleavened whole-wheat breads), although perfect for scooping up curry and dipping into the gravies, should be avoided. They are loaded with reservoirs of *ghee* (clarified butter) inside and out.

Parathas (buttered, layered unleavened flat breads) are possibly the most delicious of the Indian breads—crisp and golden brown. But because of the butter, they should also be avoided.

BUTTER, OILS, AND CREAMS

Until recently, *ghee* was the chosen cooking fat in India because it was thought to contain healthful attributes. In fact, young Indian children were given a spoonful of *ghee* daily as if it were a vitamin pill to enhance their health; but we know better now.

To stay on a healthful eating plan while eating Indian food, avoid food made with *ghee*. Indian cooks generally add a generous amount of clarified butter to *biryanis* (long-grain basmati rice dishes) right before serving them. So ask to have the butter left off your rice. If the chef won't accommodate you, order *biryanis* boiled or steamed instead.

Fortunately, health awareness is increasing among Indian restaurateurs, so healthful oils instead of butter are often used for cooking today. On request, corn, safflower, mustard or any healthful oil can easily be substituted. Mustard oil is one of the more popular healthful oils Indian chefs like to use. It's a clear or pale yellow oil made from mustard seeds that flavors fish and vegetable dishes deliciously.

Recently, a client of mine called ahead and asked the chef at her favorite Indian restaurant to take the calories out of *palak paneer*. He did, and she raved about the results. *Palak paneer* is a combination of pureed spinach and milk curd cheese. The recipe usually calls for a lot of oil and whole milk, so the chef substituted nonfat milk and reduced the oil to one tablespoon.

Other than the obsessive use of butter, oil, and whole milk, Indian food is low in fat. The meats Indian chefs commonly use are lean, and before cooking they almost always remove the skin on chicken so the spices can penetrate the meat.

Chicken, fish, lobster, and shrimp, cooked *tandoori*-style (roasted on a spit) in a *tandoor* (Indian clay oven), are delicious. They're healthful, low-fat barbecuelike dishes. They get their reddish color from the yogurt, spices, and a bright orange vegetable dye used to marinate them. Just make sure *ghee* isn't added to your *tandoori* dishes.

Curry

Curry means sauce, a sauce that can be used to flavor Indian rice, vegetable, chicken, and meat dishes. Some chefs use a premade powder to make curry, while others prefer mixing their own spices. They combine cumin, cloves, coriander, cinnamon, ginger, turmeric, and ingredients such as *chickpea* (garbanzo bean) flour, yogurt, onion, and garlic to flavor dishes however they prefer. *Curry* doesn't have to be spicy hot. Some mild curries, without the heat, are more delicious than the fiery hot ones, which may irritate your system and keep you awake at night.

Seasonings That Promote Health

Spices in India are used to flavor food, but they are also used to promote good health. Certain spices are used in the winter, others are appropriate for the hot summer months, and some—the Indians believe—prevent ailments.

In India, *masalas* is the word used to describe whole spices, most of which are not hot. They are added to Indian foods according to the taste and consistency desired.

Garam masalas are mixtures of dried spices such as coriander, cardamon, and cinnamon used to flavor a variety of Indian dishes, including curry sauces.

To make *wet masalas* (flavorful broths), water, broth, vinegar, ground coconut, or coconut milk is added to the food. Avoid dishes containing coconut, which adds a lot of unwanted fat.

Turmeric improves the appetite and acts as an antiseptic. *Asafetida* is a digestive that combats gas. Garlic is thought by some health experts to prevent colds and cancer and lower blood pressure. Order dishes containing lots of garlic often. Both garlic and onions improve circulation, provide an antibiotic effect, and some say lengthen life by decreasing cholesterol. Coriander leaves, cilantro, fenugreek, mint, clove, cardamon, nutmeg, mace, ginger, chili, and mustard seeds are common seasonings, used in India, for which there are no medicinal attributes.

Although beliefs about herbs and spices are not scientifically proven, the Indians cook with them, keeping their tastes and health benefits in mind. When eating Indian food, Indians say, you should never be aware of separate spices. Instead, a harmonious blending should come through.

Salt

You should never be aware of a salty taste when eating Indian food. Unfortunately, *dals* (pureed *pulses* lentils, split peas, and beans) used for dipping or spooning over rice are usually loaded with salt, but otherwise *dals* are extremely healthful, providing a great deal of protein and soluble fiber.

Fortunately, *dals* don't have to be salty, because in most Indian restaurants they are made to order. If there is too much salt in any dish you're served, send it back.

Paan

Paan is a digestive and breath freshener made from fresh betel leaf folded around a mixture of lime, betel nut, and spices. Most restaurateurs offer it to their guests after a meal, and Indians chew it avidly to avoid indigestion.

When it comes to *paan*, I caution my clients not to overindulge because *paan* reddens and numbs the tongue slightly. Some people find it addictive, and it can be hard on the teeth.

Indian Fast Food

If you're in a hurry, and in the mood for Indian food, here are a few fast-food suggestions available in America and India alike. *Pappadum* (crisp cracker bread made from lentil flour) is available at most Indian fast-food spots. Order it with *dal* (pureed lentils) and you'll think you're eating something that tastes a little like salt-free potato chips and dip. But only order it when it's baked in the *tandoor* and hasn't been fried.

You may be tempted to try *samosas* (delicious-tasting triangular-shaped pockets made from whole-wheat dough and filled with vegetables, meat, or cheese) or *pakoras* (vegetable fritters), but I don't recommend these fried dishes. Try a vegetable *kabab* instead—vegetables rolled in pancakelike Indian bread that looks like a rolled sandwich. At your favorite Indian fast-food restaurant, you could also order *tandoori* chicken, some rice, salad, a yogurt-based vegetable salad, and a mango *lassi* for a quick and delicious Indian meal.

▲

Taste of India Menu

I've checked off my recommendations on the Taste of India menu. This restaurant, in Sherman Oaks, California, serves many of the delicious Indian dishes you can enjoy without going off your eating plan.

Appetizers

1. Samosa
   Potatoes, and peas, and herbs and served with mint chutney.
2. Meat Samosa
   Minced lamb, peas, onions and herbs, deep fried.
3. Onion Bhaji
   Crispy onion balls deep fried.
4. Assorted Plate
   Piece of Chicken Tikka, Sheekh Kabab, Pakora, Samosa.
5. Fish Pakora
   Fish marinated in spicy herbs and deep fried to crisp golden brown.

Tandoori Oven Magic

All Tandoori dishes served hot on a bed of sauteed onions, lemon strips and mint leaves.

√ 6. Tandoori Chicken
Chicken marinated in yogurt, spices, in its juices and cooked in a clay oven.

7. Tandoori Game Hen
Wild game hen, marinated in yogurt, spices, citric juices, cooked in clay oven, on red hot charcoal.

√ 8. Chicken Tikka
Boneless pieces of chicken, marinated in yogurt, fresh spices, and juices, roasted in a clay oven.

√ 9. Reshami Kabab
Strips of white chicken breast. Prepared with special spices and herbs, roasted in a clay oven.

10. Seekh Kabab
Minced lamb meat, mixed with herbs and spices, roasted to a perfect brown on skewers over red hot charcoals, served with mint chutney and onions.

11. Lamb Tikka
Lamb pieces dipped in special marinade, then roasted Tandoori style.

12. Mixed Tandoori
An assortment of Tandoori Chicken, Chicken Tikka, Lamb Boti Kabab, Seekh Kabab.

13. Rack of Lamb
Marinated in spices cooked in clay oven over a bed of hot charcoal.

Seafood

√ 14. Shrimp Bhuna
Cooked in gently flavored, rich sauce with tomatoes, bell pepper & herbs.

15. Shrimp Saag
With fresh chopped spinach & herbs.

√ 16. Shrimp Tandoori
Jumbo Shrimps marinated in yogurt with

√ = **Recommended**

delicate spices and roasted in clay oven over red hot charcoal. A truly delightful dish.

√ 17. Shrimp/Fish Masala
Charbroiled tender, fresh shrimp/fish cooked in our special thick gravy with spices and herbs.

√ 18. Shrimp Korma
Tender, marinated shrimp spiced mildly and covered with red onions, yogurt and assorted nuts.

√ 19. Shrimp Curry
Shrimp marinated in herbs and spices and roasted tender.

Vegetarian Specialties

√ 20. Bhindi/Mushroom Bhaji
Okra/Mushroom cooked in herbs and spices with onions.

√ 21. Shimla Mirch
Two bell peppers stuffed with potatoes and spices.

22. Matar Paneer
Peas cooked with homemade cheese, in mild spices and gravy.

23. Mirchi Ka Salan [too spicy!]
Very spicy green peppers cooked in special house gravy, with herbs and spices.

√ 24. Mixed Vegetable Curry
Cooked with spices, ginger, onions and garlic.

25. Saag Paneer
Fresh spinach, cooked curry style with herbs and spice and homemade cheeses.

√ 26. Chana Masala [very healthy when not deep fried]
Chick Peas Punjabi Style.

√ 27. Alu Gobhi
Fresh cauliflower and potato curry with herbs and spices.

√ 28. Bengan Bartha
Fresh eggplant roasted in the Tandoor oven, then cooked curry style with fresh tomatoes.

√ = Recommended

29. Malai Kofta
    Vegetable balls made with deep fried vegetables, in a cream tomato and onion sauce.
30. Shahi Paneer
    Chunks of homemade cheese cooked with cream, spices, herbs and nuts.
31. Daal Makhni (Special)
    Lentils, spiced very mildly, cooked with cream and butter [order this dish if the chef will make it with little oil and no cream]

Curries

32. Chicken/Lamb Curry
    Very mildly spiced and cooked in a special gravy.

√ 33. Chicken Tikka Masala
    Boneless Chicken baked in a clay oven, then cooked in a special curry sauce in the Tandoor.

√ 34. Chicken Vindaloo
    Chicken pieces and potatoes cooked with spices and tomatoes.

35. Karahai Chicken or Chicken Madras
    Chicken pieces cooked in butter and served in a tomato gravy.
36. Chicken Saag Wala (Chicken Spinach)
    Chicken pieces cooked with special spices and served with creamy spinach curry.
37. Chicken Makhni
    Tandoori Chicken cooked in butter and served in a tomato gravy.
38. Chicken Murg Masala
    Chicken cooked in traditional Indian sauce enhanced with eggs.
39. Chicken Korma
    Chicken pieces spiced mildly and cooked with onions, yogurt, cream and nuts.

√ 40. Chicken Jalphearezi
    Boneless chicken cooked with mixed vegetables.

√ = Recommended

41. Lamb Vindaloo
    Lamb cooked with special spices and potatoes in a thick gravy.
42. Saag Lela (Lamb spinach)
    Lamb cooked in special spices, served in a cream and spinach gravy.
43. Lamb Dopiaza
    Lamb cooked with brown onions in a special gravy. Mildly spicy.
44. Lamb Shahi Korma
    Marinated lamb cooked with onion, yogurt, cream and assorted nuts. Mildly spicy.
45. Rogan Josh
    Lamb pieces cooked in a tomato and onion sauce.
46. Keema Mattar
    Finely minced lamb, cooked with herbs, spices and green peas.
47. Lamb Bhuna
    Lamb pieces spiced mildly and cooked in a tomato gravy with extra garlic and ginger.

Biryanis

Exciting Rice Introductions [NOTE: Ask if they can make them without butter.]

48. Shrimp Biryanis
    Fresh Shrimp cooked with aromatic rice, almonds and flavored with saffron.
49. Lamb Biryanis
    Aromatic Basmati Rice cooked with pieces of lamb and a special blend of herbs and spices.
50. Chicken Biryanis
    Aromatic Basmati Rice cooked with pieces of chicken and a special blend of herbs and spices.
51. Vegetable Biryanis
    Aromatic Basmati Rice cooked with garden fresh vegetables, herbs and spices.

√ = **Recommended**

√ 52. Plain Rice
Steamed Basmati Rice.

Tandoori Breads

√ Chapati Tandoori
Indian style basic whole wheat bread.

√ Naan
Indian style plain leavened whole wheat bread.

Paratha
Indian style multi-layered whole wheat bread, topped with butter.

√ Onion Kulcha
A North Indian specialty Naan stuffed with onions, seasoned in mild mint sauce.

Keema Naan
Naan stuffed with delicately spiced Sheekh Kabab.

√ Garlic Naan
Naan stuffed with fresh garlic.

Alu Paratha
Paratha stuffed with spiced, mashed potatoes and peas.

Gobhi Paratha
Paratha stuffed with spiced minced cauliflower.

Desserts

Rasmalai
Our own freshly made soft cheese patties, drenched in thick, sweet milk, laced with grated pistachios, served chilled.

Gulab Jamun
Freshly made savory cheese balls, deep fried to a rosy brown in purified butter and gently cooked in light, rose flavored syrup.

Mango Ice Cream
Prepared with choice mango pulp.

Rice Pudding
Basmati rice cooked with sweet milk and cream, nuts and raisins.

√ = Recommended

Kulfi

Pistachio Ice Cream.

Beverages

Milk

Soft Drinks

√ Indian Tea (hot)

√ Lassi

√ Mango Lassi

√ Iced Tea

√ Perrier Water

√ Coffee

Beer Domestic

Beer Imported

Indian: Taj, King Fisher, Golden

Heineken, Corona, Becks

Wine Rośe, Chablis, Burgundy

(Please Specify When Ordering: Mild, Medium or Spicy.)

▼

√ = Recommended

✓TO CHOOSE

Take this Menu Command along—as your guide—and avoid the butter, salt, and sugar in your favorite Indian dishes.

Drinks (Paibadhart)

Beers: drink Indian beers such as King Fisher or Taj Mahal in moderation, diet permitting; they don't contain sulfites
Istanbuli tea: order the herbal variety
Juices: apple, orange, mango
Lassi drink (yogurt, pureed fruit—mango or lychee nut—and water): order the nonalcoholic variety
Kafi (coffee): contains caffeine; drink in moderation
Limboo pani (lime water): an alternative to water that goes well with curry; it's an appetite stimulant
Mineral waters
Pani (water)
Ruafsa (pink cordial syrup added to water): enjoy if your diet permits sugar
Soft drinks flavored with fruits and vegetables; mango sodas are delicious

***Choose* drinks that don't contain caffeine or excessive amounts of sugar.**
***BEST BETS*: Mineral waters, *limboo pani*, or *lassi* (nonalcoholic varieties are recommended)**

Appetizers (Shuruat)

Chicken *kabab* (ground chicken mixed with yogurt and spices): very popular
Kashk-e-badamjan (sautéed eggplant and onions topped with yogurt)
Tandoori mixed grill (chicken and fish cooked on a stick in the *tandoor*)

✓TO CHOOSE

Choose **appetizers that are not fried or made with butter.**
BEST BETS: Kashk-e-badamjan **or** ***tandoori*** **mixed grill.**

Soups (Rase-ki-sabgi)

Chicken soup: clear and defatted
Dal soup (pureed lentils and vegetables)
Mixed vegetable soup
Mulligatawny (lentil soup delicately seasoned): usually made with defatted broth base
Sambar (a mixture of diced vegetables, split peas, and lentils)

Choose **Indian soups often; they're delicious and healthful.**
BEST BETS: dal **soup or** ***mulligatawny***

Tandoori Dishes (Cooked in Clay Oven)

Chicken *tikka* (chicken pieces mesquite-broiled and roasted)
Dahi chicken (*tandoori* chicken)
Fish *tikka* (whitefish marinated in yogurt, Indian spices, and then cooked in the *tandoori* oven)
Murghi tandoori (half Cornish hen broiled in *tandoor*)
Pomfret (Bombay fish similar to sole)
Shrimp *tikka* (pieces of marinated shrimp): fried
Tandoori chicken (chicken marinated in yogurt)
Tandoori filet (chunks of filet mignon with onions, green peppers, and spices)
Tandoori lobster (lobster marinated in flavorful spices and roasted in the *tandoor*)
Tandoori shrimp (shrimp marinated in yogurt and roasted in the clay oven)

✓ To Choose

***Choose* dishes cooked in the *tandoor*; it's a healthful way of cooking that keeps food juicy.**
***BEST BETS: Tandoori* chicken, *tandoori* filet, or *tandoori* lobster**

Curries (Rasam)

Bhuna chicken (boneless chicken cooked in yogurt, sliced onions, and a variety of spices)
Chicken curry (chicken cooked with tomatoes, onions, garlic, and spices)
Chicken *jalfrezi* (boneless pieces of chicken cooked with onions, capsicum, ginger, and tomatoes)
Chicken *sagwala* (chicken and spinach cooked with spices in a curry sauce)
Chicken *tikka* (chicken broiled on a skewer)
Chicken *vindaloo* (boneless chicken in a tangy sauce): if you can tolerate spices
Fish *goa* (marinated with ginger, garlic, spiced yogurt, and cooked in a tangy sauce)
Fish *masala* (fish cubes cooked in gravy)
Karahi chicken (boneless chicken stir-fried with bell pepper, onions, and tomatoes)
Lobster *bhuna* (lobster cooked in flavorful curry gravy)
Macchi patiala (fish prepared with curry gravy)
Prawn *bhuna* (prawns in curry gravy)
Shahi kofta (Indian-style meatballs cooked in curry sauce)
Shrimp in green *masala* (shrimp cooked in green spices)

***Choose* curry dishes made without butter and those that aren't too spicy for your digestive system.**
BEST BETS*: Chicken curry, fish *masala*, or *shahi kofta

✓To Choose

Vegetarian Dishes (Bahar-e-sabaz)

Aloo gobi (potatoes and cauliflower sautéed with mild spices)
Aloo matar (peas cooked with potatoes and tomatoes)
Aloo palak (spinach and potatoes)
Aloo phalian (French beans and potatoes sautéed in spices)
Baigan bartha (eggplant baked with onions and tomatoes and spices)
Bartha (roasted eggplant curry)
Bhindi masala (fresh okra sautéed with onions and spices)
Chana masala (garbanzos cooked in tomato sauce with herbs and spices)
Chana mushroom (mushrooms and chickpea curry)
Jaipuri masala (seasonal vegetables in sauce)
Matar paneer (cubed farmer's cheese and green peas in a spiced gravy)
Mushroom *matar* (mushrooms and peas braised with mild spices)
Raita (raw vegetables chopped and mixed with yogurt)
Sai bhaji (vegetable-legume dish eaten with rice)
Sangam bhaji (mixed vegetable curry)
Vegetable *kurma* (mixed vegetables cooked with yogurt)
Vegetable *malai kofta* (vegetables cooked on a stick)
Vegetable *thali* (platter of vegetable dishes, rice, bread, and condiments): request vegetables without butter or cream
Zaffrani dal (washed lentils cooked with spices and saffron)

Choose **vegetable dishes made without butter or cream.**
BEST BETS: Aloo gobi **or** ***baigan bartha***

✓TO CHOOSE

Rice Specialties (Inam)

Basmati rice (an expensive long-grain rice): often colored
Guchhi plillau (rice cooked with mushrooms)
Methi rice (basmati rice cooked with fenugreek leaves)
Peas *pillau* (rice cooked with peas and spices)
Plain steamed rice
Pudina pillau (rice cooked with mint, cilantro, and hot chilies)
Vegetable *pillau* (basmati rice and vegetables cooked together)

***Choose* rice dishes that aren't made with butter.**
***BEST BETS*: peas *pillau* or plain steamed rice**

Indian Bread (Roti)

Aloo (*naan* filled with peas and potatoes)
Chapati (unleavened whole-wheat pancakelike bread)
Dosa (paper-thin pancake bread made from lentil flour and water)
Garlic *naan* (leavened white flour bread topped with fresh garlic)
Idli (soft steamed rice cakes)
Masala osa (bread wrapped around curried vegetables)
Naan (white flour bread freshly baked in the *tandoor*)
Onion *kulcha naan* (white flat bread stuffed with onions)
Paaw (roll found in India)
Paneer naan (cheese and spices cooked inside *naan*)
Pappadum (lentil wafers): order when not fried in oil; Indian people crush them over their food.
Vegetarian *naan* (*naan* filled with vegetables)

✓ TO CHOOSE

***Choose* Indian breads that haven't been fried or topped with butter.**
BEST BETS: Chapati*, garlic *naan*, or onion *kulcha naan

Side Dishes (Kuch-Aur-Chatbati Chija)

Chutney (pureed fruit and vegetable made into a sauce)
Dal makhany (lentils in spices)
Mint *chutney*
Raita (yogurt with cucumber and herbs)

***Choose* Indian condiments; they're delicious and healthful.**
***BEST BETS: Dal makhany, raita*, or chutney**

Sweet Dishes (Methai)

Lassi (mango or lichee nut yogurt drink)
Mango
Phal (fruit)
Shrikand: contains sugar, but not too much.

***Choose* fresh fruit for dessert.**
BEST BET: Lassi* or *phal

⊘ TO AVOID

Drinks

Alcoholic beverages
Arrack (alcoholic drinks made with coconut milk)
Chai tea: most Indian teas contain caffeine
Tap water: should be avoided in India

⊘ TO AVOID

Thandai (sweet drink made with milk, nuts, and spices)
Wines: most Indian wines contain sulfites

Avoid beverages that contain sugar, caffeine, or sulfites.

Appetizers

Chana ki dal (deep-fried, spiced chickpeas): eaten like nuts
Chicken *chat* (chicken mixed with potatoes and sweet-and-sour sauce)
Chicken *pakoras* (fried chicken pieces)
Kaleji kababs (chicken livers on a stick): organ meats are high in cholesterol
Pakora murgh (battered deep-fried chicken)
Pakoras (fried mixed vegetable fritters dusted with garbanzo bean flour, which makes them puffy)
Samosa (deep-fried triangular-shaped dough filled with vegetables, and sometimes meat or cheese)
Shrimp *chat* (shrimps in sweet-and-sour sauce)
Vegetable *pakora* (cauliflower and potato fritter fried in butter)

***Avoid* appetizers that are fried and those made with sweet sauces.**

Soups

Creamy chicken soup: usually too fatty
Rasam (spicy soup): usually too spicy

***Avoid* soups that are creamed or too spicy for your digestive system.**

⊘TO AVOID

Tandoori Dishes

Chicken roll: fried
Keema mattar (finely minced lamb cooked with herbs, peas, and potatoes)
Lamb roll: fried
Lamb *tikka*: lamb is too fatty

***Avoid* fried *tandoori* dishes and those made with lamb; they are too fatty.**

Curry Dishes

Chicken *jalfrezi* (chicken with vegetables, seasonings, and topped with cheese)
Chicken *makhanwala* (shredded *tandoori* chicken in a sauce of butter, tomatoes, and spices)
Chicken *sagwala* (chicken cooked with spiced creamed spinach)
Crab *kofta malai* (crab cooked in nuts, cream, and seasonings)
Lamb *korma* (cubes of lamb in spices and cream)
Mutter paneer (Indian cream cheese and peas)
Rogham josh (curried lamb dish made with thick, red sauce)
Saag lamb (cooked with spices, creamed spinach, and ginger)
Shrimp and green mango curry: contains grated coconut in addition to coconut milk; a basically saturated fat.

***Avoid* highly spiced curries, unless your stomach can handle them, and those made with lamb or pork; they're too fatty.**

⊘ To Avoid

Vegetarian Dishes

Bartha (eggplant baked and sautéed with onions, herbs, and cream)
Bhajria (flat fritters made of flour, spices, and vegetables): fried
Dal makhani (creamed lentils)
Dal palak (washed creamed lentils prepared with spinach)
Navrattan korma (vegetables cooked in mild cream sauce with spices)
Pulao (rice fried in *ghee* and then cooked in stock)
Saag paneer (homemade cheese cubes cooked with spinach)

***Avoid* fried vegetarian dishes and those made with cream, butter, or cheese.**

Rice Specialties

Chicken *biryani* (chicken, rice, vegetables, and butter)
Moghlai biryani (diced chicken in a blend of herbs with basmati rice)
Mutton *biryani* (basmati rice flavored with lamb, butter, saffron, nuts, eggs, and other spices)
Seafood *biryani* (seafood blended with spices)
Vegetable *biryani* (rice, vegetables, and butter)

***Avoid* rice dishes made with butter or lamb.**

Indian Bread

Aloo paratha (whole-wheat buttered bread stuffed with potatoes, peas, and spices)
Egg naan (bread made with eggs)

⊘TO AVOID

Keema naan (white bread stuffed with ground lamb, herbs, and spices)
Paratha (fried bread made from whole-wheat flour and butter)
Puri (deep-fried *chapati*)

***Avoid* bread fried in oil and those topped with butter.**

Side Dishes

Achars (pickles): too salty and spicy
Coconut chutney

***Avoid* condiments that are loaded with sugar or pickled in salt.**

Desserts

Barfi (bars made from condensed milk sweetened with ground almonds, pistachio nuts, and cardamon)
Gajar halwa (carrot cream dessert)
Gulab jamun (cream cheese balls made with dry milk balls and sweet rose-water syrup): they swell and are spongy
Khajoor (Indian doughnuts)
Kheer (sweet rice pudding made with milk, nuts, and rose water)
Kulfi (Indian ice cream made with pistachio, saffron, and nuts): mango is a popular flavor
Rusgoola (little balls of cream floating in rose water): similar to *gulab jamun*
Rusmalai (Indian cream cheese in sweetened milk and pistachios): the supreme creamy dessert

***Avoid* desserts loaded with sugar and butter.**

Indian Defensive Dining Tips

These eight tips will help you choose wisely when eating Indian cuisine:

1. Eat moderate first servings since Indian people consider it impolite if you don't take second helpings. With the first serving, your waiter will think you're merely determining which foods you like best.
2. Eat plenty of yogurt with your curry dishes, and ask the chef for *boily* foods (unspiced steamed dishes) made without red, green, or cayenne peppers if they upset your stomach. Most Indians are not bothered by indigestion, but those who are eat *boily* foods regularly.
3. Unless the chef will omit the butter, stop eating ***biryanis*** and order plain steamed rice instead.
4. Don't eat anything made with *ghee*. If you see or taste butter in a dish, send it back.
5. Avoid excessively salty dishes.
6. Order à la carte. That way it's easier to fit healthful foods into your eating plan.
7. Eat *tandoori*-style fish and chicken dishes more often.
8. Chew on *paan* after meals; it may be psychological, but your stomach may be thankful afterward!

Indian Phrases

The following requests will help if the menu you're ordering from isn't in English and you want something made a special way.

1. **I'd like a cup of lentil soup.**
   Mera eik cup soup chotta hai.

2. **Please bring me two fresh vegetable dishes made without butter, cream, or cheese.**
Muje dho vegetable chahiya bina butter, cream, cheese.

3. **I'd like some a. fish, or b. chicken, *tandoori* style.**
Muje a. machi, or b. murghi, tandoori chahiya.

4. **Please bring me a. fish, or b. chicken, cooked in curry and seasoned d. mild, e. medium, or f. hot.**
Muje a. fish, or b. chicken, curry chahiya d. masala math dalo, e. thora se masala dalo, f. ziada masala dalo.

5. **I'd like steamed rice combined with vegetables.**
Muje rice and vegetables chahiya.

6. **Please bring me an order of *naan* a. plain, or topped with b. garlic, or c. onion.**
Mujee a. naan, b. garlic naan, c. onion naan chahiya.

7. **I'd like some *dal, chutney*, and other condiments you recommend with my meal.**
Muje dal, chutney, raita, achar, chahiya.

8. **Please bring me a dish of fresh fruit for dessert.**
Fruit dish laye.

9. **I'd like a cup of herbal Istanbuli tea.**
Muje Istanbuli chai chahiya.

10. **All I need now is the check. Thanks.**
Mera bill please. Shukria.

THE BOTTOM LINE

To lose weight and stay on your eating plan while eating Indian food, it's not only what you eat, but how much that matters. Eating moderate portions can be difficult in Indian restaurants because more food is presented than you can possibly eat.

Although most Indian food is delicious, all restaurants are

not considered equal. Restaurants are graded, similar to the way we grade our hotels, one, two, and three. Their ratings are usually displayed on the outside of the building—three is the worst, two is in the middle, and one is the best. Particularly avoid the cold food served at grade three restaurants, usually found at railway or bus stations, because it may not be hygienic. A cup of hot tea or something else hot that has been cooked well will probably be safe, however.

You'll have to use your own judgment about whether or not to eat at a grade two Indian restaurant. If you walk into one that doesn't look clean, leave. Your concerns will disappear when you enter a grade one. You'll hear the melodic music, enjoy the aromas, and see the beautiful seating arrangements. The unique blending of herbs, yogurt, meats, vegetables, dried beans, split peas, and lentils make Indian cuisine one of the most interesting in the world.

In the next chapter, you will learn how to incorporate Greek food into your healthful way of eating.

Bojhan khushise khaleh! (Enjoy yourselves!)

Chapter 11

▲

GREEK FOOD

THE Greeks think of life as tragic, sweet brevity. They are willing to accept the worst about life, so they can also accept the best. They have a love affair with food, think of it as one of life's greatest pleasures, and look forward to mealtime. For the most part, the Greek cuisine is a healthy one. Greek people love simply prepared dishes made from the freshest, most healthful ingredients. They have a vital understanding of what food should taste like, because most of what they eat is organically grown and flavorful.

GREEK REGIONAL COOKING

Throughout Greece, the dishes are pretty much the same, but the ingredients vary. Since transportation is poor, chefs must cook with whatever is available to them. They depend upon the fish from the Mediterranean Sea and the organically grown fruits and vegetables from the ground.

A greater variety of fruits and vegetables grow in the north because the soil is richer there. The south is arid, for the most part, so a lot of food that is eaten in the south comes from the sea.

Meat

Because farm and grazing land is scarce, meat is at a premium throughout Greece. The farmers have learned that more people can be fed when the little fertile ground they have is used to grow plants rather than raise animals, so there isn't much beef, butter, cream, lamb, or veal available in Greece.

Most people think Greeks eat primarily lamb for protein, but lamb is available in Greece only in the spring, not year round. And, because lamb is high in fat, I suggest you avoid it—even when it is on the menu. Fresh seafood, chicken, and goat meat—available in Greece year round—are the sources of animal protein I recommend most because they are lean.

Cheese

Feta (a white, crumbly, salty cheese made from goat's milk) is used in many Greek dishes, but mainly in salads. *Kasseri* (a firm golden cheese) is eaten fresh, grated over macaroni, or fried. Although these cheeses are delicious, they are salty, fatty, and not a dieter's food.

Every island in Greece makes its own cheese. Their creaminess is determined by the type of milk that was obtainable.

Popular Dishes

Mousaka (eggplant, cheese, ground meat) and *pastistio* (pasta, ground meat) are popular dishes throughout Greece. They are baked with *béchamel* (a creamy white sauce made from flour, butter, milk) and usually too much *lathi* (olive oil) or butter. Depending upon the time of the year and the ingredients available, ***mousaka*** is made with eggplant, potatoes, or zucchini. Popular dishes I recommend include ***kotopoulo lemonato*** (chicken fillets on a skewer, marinated in lemon juice, olive oil, and herbs), ***psarosoupa*** (a ***bouillabaisse***like soup), and ***dolmathes*** (grape leaves filled with rice and ground meat).

Oils and Fats

It's only when olive oil, ***béchamel*** sauce, or butter are used excessively that the average Greek diet contains too much fat. Other than ***béchamel***, Greek people don't like gravies or cream sauces.

Greeks eat lightly, season their food with spices such as nutmeg, cinnamon, allspice, and aniseed, cook with moderate amounts of olive oil, and enjoy an abundance of fresh fruits and vegetables. The flavors blend magnificently.

Vegetables

In addition to eggplant, potatoes, zucchini, peppers, onions, tomatoes, string beans, okra, artichokes, and vegetables used to make salads, the Greeks eat ***horta*** (vegetables such as Swiss chard, dandelion greens, or mustard greens) at both lunch and dinner. These greens are loaded with vitamins and minerals, and cooked slowly, without a lot of water, to preserve their nutritional value.

Horta is available in most Greek restaurants, since people in Greece rely on fresh vegetables for a great deal of their nourishment.

TRADITIONAL GREEK DINING

Since Greek people like to eat simple foods, they eat a light ***proyevma*** (breakfast), the way appetizers are eaten in other countries. Their largest meal, *yevma* (lunch), is served between 12:30 and 3:00 P.M. Another light meal is *vrathinoyevma* (dinner), beginning in winter around 7:30 P.M. and in the summer continuing until 1:00 A.M.

Most Greek people have a sweet tooth, but they end their meals with fresh fruits instead of rich desserts. Grapes, apricots, melons, peaches, apples, and tangerines are some of the more popular fruits Greeks enjoy. Seasonal fruits are enjoyed regularly, too.

Baklava, and all the other sweet pastries Greeks are known for, are generally enjoyed a couple of hours before dinner. Then, immediately before the meal, *mezethes* (Greek appetizers) are eaten.

The Greeks don't need fancy foods. They cut up a cucumber and tomato, top them with a little *feta* cheese, olive oil, rosemary, and that's a meal. Each item is so delectable, they don't need anything else. They simmer seasonal vegetables in a *tapsio* (a big pot). The vegetables they use depend upon what's in season at that time of year. The Greeks pickle their own olives and make their own bread and cheese (watch out for the olives, they contain a lot of salt and fat!).

Lunchtime is observed no matter what else is going on, because lunch is more than a meal; it is a ceremony. Greek people like to take a nap after they eat or possibly make love and then sleep. At one time the government tried to change the Greek lunchtime to a Western schedule to increase productivity, but the people rebelled and wouldn't allow it.

Most Greek people still don't have televisions, so they provide their own entertainment by going to three or four restaurants instead of one for their entire meal. They start out at one restaurant for appetizers, then go to another for the main course, and perhaps a third for dessert. This custom allows Greek restaurateurs to specialize.

After dinner, Greeks promenade. They want to see each other and show off their families. In the spring or summer, when the weather is nice, it's common to see an entire family strolling together at midnight.

Not many restaurants in Greece serve foods from distant lands, because the Greeks aren't easily influenced and enjoy their own cuisine best.

GREEK DINING EXPERIENCE

Whenever I think about Greek food, I remember a Greek dinner I was invited to. Every item served was a complement to a healthful diet.

We started with ***kouloura*** (a delicious soft bread covered with sesame seeds). At the same time the waiters brought us small bowls filled with ***taramousalata*** (pureed red caviar) and ***tsasiki*** (yogurt, cucumber sauce). We dipped small pieces of bread into the side dishes as violins played in the background.

Next came appetizer-size servings of ***kalamaria Alexandra*** (stuffed squid) and ***garithes*** (large baked butterfly shrimp). Each was covered with a different but equally delicious, fresh tomato-based sauce, so pure and delicious they tasted like pureed vegetable soup. The squid reminded me of stuffed pasta shells both in appearance and taste. The waiter said they had been cleaned, boiled, and steamed, before being baked, so they were tender enough to cut with a fork. The shrimp tasted a lot like lobster.

Before I could finish, the waiters brought in ***horiatiki*** (village salad made of chopped cucumber, red onion, peppers, tomato, black olives, and a little ***feta*** cheese). I was satisfied after eating the appetizers and salad, but they were merely the beginning of our feast.

Steamed fresh green beans and thick julienne-style carrots, a mound of ***horta salata*** (steamed greens sautéed in a little olive oil with rice and onions), came next. The vegetables were followed by a thick piece of halibut covered with sauce made from tomatoes stewed with parsley, bay leaf, and garlic.

At the end of the meal, the music got louder as the waiters joined arms. They performed the traditional dances of Greece until we were all dancing. Greek food and singing and dancing to the Greek music was a delight to our senses.

Greek Fast Food

The cuisines of Greece, Turkey, Lebanon, Syria, Jordan, Iraq, Israel, Persia, and Egypt overlap, making up what is known as Middle Eastern or Mediterranean food. Although distinct in many ways, the people from these nine countries are bound together by certain foods.

For example, spinach is *spanaki* in Greek, *ispanak* in Turkish, and *esfanaj* in Persian. Eggplant is *melitzana* in Greece, *bademjan* in Persia, and *badinjan* in Lebanon. These foods and others are used to make healthful Middle Eastern dishes that can be prepared ahead of time and served fast, such as *tabbouleh* (wheat, tomato, mint, and parsley salad), *falafel* (bean croquette sandwich), and *hummus* (pureed chickpea spread); delightful with *pita* bread. Avoid *gyros* (lamb and beef pressed together and cooked on a rotisserie) and *tahina* (ground sesame seeds) because these items contain too much fat for anyone trying to lose weight.

▲

Papadakis Taverna Menu

On request, the chefs at Papadakis Taverna, in San Pedro, California, will modify the ingredients and turn typically fatty Greek dishes into healthful ones. They'll make *spanakopita* (spinach-cheese pie) without cheese or butter and use moderate amounts of olive oil instead. They'll make a delicious-tasting vegetarian *mousaka* (eggplant casserole) with or without *béchamel* sauce. **I've checked off the more healthful items.**

Appetizers

Assortments available

KEFTETHES lamb meatballs

SAGANAKI flamed kasseri cheese

GARITHO FILO shrimp, kassari, tomato in pastry

√ DOLMATHES stuffed grape leaves [order only if vegetarian style]

√ KALAMARIA ALEXANDRA stuffed squid

√ GARITHES baked shrimp

LUKANIKO Greek pork sausage

√ OCTOPOTHI LEMONATO octopus salad

√ HORTA SALATA fresh boiled greens

√ GARITHO SALATA shrimp salad

√ TASOS SALATA village salad

TERI ELYES assorted Greek cheese with olives

TIROPITA cheeses baked in filo

SPANAKOPITA spinach baked in filo

KREATOPITA chopped lamb baked in filo

ANGINARES artichoke hearts with cheese baked in filo

COMBINATION one piece of each filo baked pastries

Dinners: taramousalata, tsasiki, soup and salad, kouloura

KEFTETHES lamb meatballs on a bed of pilaf, herbed sauce

ARNI FRIKASE lamb braised with artichoke, avgolemono

ARNI ALA PAPADAKIS Saddle of lamb in pastry (original)

√ KAVOURI MOUSTARTHA king crab leg in pastry and mustard sauce (original)

GARITHES GLIFATHA shrimp baked in tomatoes, wine, feta

MOUSHARI VASSILIKO white veal filets with kasseri in pastry and basil sauce (original)

√ KOTA STI SKARA boneless chicken breast marinated and char-broiled

√ KOTA KEFALONIA boneless chicken breast in pastry (original)

√ = Recommended

√ PSARI PLAKI filet of sea bass baked (in season only)
√ KSIFIAS STI SKARA swordfish grilled with herbs (in season only)
PAITHAKIA STI SKARA loin lamb chops char-broiled
STEFANA ARNI rack of lamb
FILETO saddle of lamb char-broiled
BRIZOLA center cut New York steak char-broiled
MOUSHARI STI SKARA white veal loin chop char-broiled
SOUFLAKI loin lamb skewered and char-broiled
MOUSAKA eggplant, cheese, ground lamb baked with crema béchamel
PASTISTIO pasta, ground lamb baked with crema béchamel
DOLMATHES grape leaves stuffed with lamb, pine nuts
√ KOTA KOKINISTO boneless chicken breast simmered in light herbs
COMBINATION offering mousaka, pastistio, dolma, kotopoulo, keftede

▼

√ = **Recommended**

✓TO CHOOSE

Try the "Best Bets" in every category below in your favorite Greek restaurants.

Drinks (Rofimata)

Gala (milk)
Mineral waters: Nigrita, Saniza, Loutrakiou
Nero (water)

Choose nonalcoholic beverages.
BEST BET: mineral water

Appetizers (Mezethes)

Anginares (artichoke hearts): request when made without cheese
Dolmathes (stuffed grape leaves): request if made without lamb
Kalamaria Alexandra (stuffed squid): poached
Octopothi (octopus): hung out to soften, pounded against stones, then cut into small pieces and grilled
Octopothi lemonato (octopus salad)
Satziki (yogurt, cucumber, garlic mixture)
Tahina (a dip made of ground sesame seeds, lemon juice, oil, and garlic): usually served with warm *pita*
Taramousalata (fish roe processed to a paste with garlic, bread crumbs and lemon juice): served as a dip
Tsasiki (yogurt and garlic cucumber dip)

***Choose* appetizers made from fresh ingredients that aren't fried.**
BEST BETS: dolmathes, taramousalata,* and *tsasiki

Soups (Soupes)

✓TO CHOOSE

Fahki (lentil soup)
Fassolada (bean soup)
Psarosoupa (fish, seasonings, and vegetables): introduced by the Greeks to the French, who added saffron and renamed it *bouillabaisse.*

***Choose* homemade soups made with fresh ingredients.**
BEST BET: psarosoupa

Breads (Psomi)

Kouloura (Greek bread)
Pita bread (unleavened flat pocket bread)

***Choose* Greek breads often, they're delicious.**
***BEST BET: pita* bread**

Salads and Vegetables (Salates, Lahanika)

Aegean kalamari, elbow pasta, fresh tomatoes, and garlic marinated in dressing of olive oil, cilantro, and lemon juice)
Bamyes (okra): known as ladies' fingers
Diafora salata (mixed salad)
Garitho salata (shrimp salad)
Horiatiki salata (beefsteak tomatoes, onion, *feta* cheese, olives)
Horta salata (fresh boiled greens): olive oil, lemon juice dressing; optional
Melitzana (diced eggplant and fresh bell peppers sautéed in a little olive oil)
Octopothi lemonato (octopus salad)
Patzari (boiled fresh beets sliced into a mixture of yogurt, olive oil, vinegar, garlic, and walnuts)

✓ TO CHOOSE

Prassini (green salad made with seasonal vegetables and topped with dill-lemon dressing)
Radikia (dandelion leaves): eaten with olive oil and lemon juice dressing
Tabouli (cracked wheat, fresh lemon juice, parsley, green onions, spices, tomato)
Tzatziki (yogurt and cucumber dressed with olive oil, vinegar, garlic, dill, and other spices)

***Choose* fresh salads and vegetables that contain no more than moderate amounts of oil, cheese, or olives.**
BEST BETS: horta salata, octopothi lemonato,* and *tabouli

Entrées (Keria Piata)

Barbouni (grilled red mullet fish)
Bourtheto (fish simmered with pureed onions and tomatoes)
Garithes glifatha (shrimp poached in tomatoes, wine, and a little *feta*)
Kalamari (squid): poached
Kavouri moustartha (king crab leg in pastry with mustard sauce)
Kota kokinisto (boneless chicken herbs simmered in herbs)
Kota sti skara (boneless chicken breast marinated and char-broiled)
Kotopoulo lemonato (chicken fillets on skewers marinated in lemon juice, olive oil, and herbs)
Ksifias sti skara (swordfish grilled with herbs)
Orzr pasta (pasta shaped like rice)
Pastitsatha (veal braised with tomatoes served with macaroni)
Psari marinata (marinated sardines)

✓To Choose

Psari plaki (braised or baked fish served with vegetables)
Salonika shrimp (shrimp cooked with fresh tomatoes, dill, garlic, and *feta* cheese on a bed of *orzo* pasta)
Soupya (baby squid simmered in thick tomato sauce)
Souvlaki (marinated meat on skewers): known as *kebabs*; choose beef and avoid lamb
Stifado (Greek beef stew made with tomatoes and onions)
Yemisto (bell pepper stuffed with lean ground beef, parsley, and rice): avoid when this dish is made with lamb

***Choose* main courses that don't contain lamb or a lot of cheese or oil.**
BEST BETS: Choose kalamari, kotopoulo lemonato,* and *psari plaki

Desserts (Epidorpia)

Frouta (fruit): the Greeks consider iced fresh fruit the perfect ending to a healthy meal
Karidomelo (yogurt placed in a shallow bowl, drained, crisscrossed with Greek honey, and sprinkled with chopped walnuts topped with dribbles of Greek honey)
Paxos (cinnamon *pita*)
Sliced oranges: naval oranges are popular along the Athenian district of Kolonaki

***Choose* desserts made with fresh fruit but not too much sugar.**
BEST BETS: frouta* and *paxos

⊘ TO AVOID

Drinks

Brandies: Achaia Clauss, Cambas, Metaxas, and Sans Rival
Byres (beers): Fix, Spartan, Agean
Citro (Greek liqueur)
Kafes (coffee): Greek coffee contains too much caffeine
Masticha (clear liqueur)
Ouzo (aniseed-flavored liquor): the national beverage ranges from 80 to 100 proof; don't drink it often.
Retsina (Greek wines): Patraika, Cambas, and Achaia Clauss are popular brands
Vermouths: Cinzáno, Bóthys

***Avoid* alcoholic beverages, unless your diet permits in moderation.**

Appetizers

Anginares (artichoke hearts with cheese baked in phyllo and served with lemon and herbs): avoid when baked in phyllo
Garitho filo (shrimp, *kasseri*, tomato in pastry)
Keftethes (meatballs): avoid when fried or made from lamb
Kreatopita (chopped lamb baked in phyllo)
Lukaniko (a fat, spicy red Greek sausage made from minced lamb)
Melitzanes tyganites (fried eggplant)
Saganaki (flaming *kasseri* cheese with lemon)
Tiri elyes (assorted Greek cheeses and *calamata* olives)
Tiropita (cheese baked in phyllo)

⊘TO AVOID

Avoid **appetizers containing lamb, a lot of oil or cheese, those that are fried, or made with phyllo. (Dishes made with phyllo also contain butter.)**

Soups

Avgolemono (chicken, rice, egg-lemon soup)
Mageritsa (traditional Easter soup made of heart, lungs, liver, and intestines of lamb): organ meats are loaded with cholesterol
Patsas soupa (tripe and lamb's-feet soup)

Avoid **soups made with eggs or organ meats.**

Salads and Vegetables

Kreatopita (meat, lamb, beef, and sometimes cheese in pastry)
Patates yemistes me loukanika (potatoes stuffed with sausages)
Spanakopita (phyllo pastry and spinach): served as an appetizer, vegetable, or main dish; contains a lot of butter

Avoid **salads made with a lot of cheese, oil, or butter.**

Cheese and Cheese Dishes

Feta (made from goat, sheep, or cow's milk): eat only in moderation; too salty
Gravieri (rich, creamy cheese): often served with fruit at the end of a meal
Kopanisti (blue cheese)

⊘ To Avoid

Myzithra (made from whey drained away while making *feta*)
Saganaki (thick slices of floured and fried *kasseri* cheese)

Entrées

Arni bouti (leg of lamb)
Arni frikase (spring lamb casserole)
Barbouni tiyanito (fried red mullet fish usually served with French fries): too fatty
Brizola (New York steak char-broiled): too fatty
Fileto (saddle of lamb char-broiled)
Kleftiko arni (lamb cooked in parchment paper): invented by Greek freedom fighters to prevent Turks from smelling their food and locating their hideouts.
Kokoretsi (*shish kebab* of lamb's liver, kidney, sweetbreads, and heart, wrapped in intestines and grilled): organ meats are high in cholesterol
Kreatopita (ground lamb, mushrooms, onions, pine nuts, lemon juice, cinnamon, and fresh pepper)
Mousaka (sautéed eggplant with ground beef, fresh parsley, onions, peppers, herbs, olive oil, tomato juice, and topped with *béchamel* sauce)
Moushari sti skara (veal chop char-broiled): too fatty
Paiythakia sti skara (loin lamb chops char-broiled)
Pastistio (pasta and mushrooms sautéed in butter with *béchamel* sauce and three types of Greek cheeses)
Souflaki (loin lamb skewered and char-broiled)
Stefana arni (rack of lamb)
Vegetarian mousaka (layers of eggplant and zucchini topped with *béchamel* sauce): sauce is too fatty
Youvetsi (lamb and *orzo* pasta in tomato and herb sauce, sprinkled with *kefalotiri* cheese and baked in the oven)

⊘ TO AVOID

Avoid **entrées made with lamb, fatty cuts of veal, or a lot of cheese, butter, or oil.**

Sauces

Avgolemono (egg-lemon soup): used as a sauce
Béchamel sauce (flour, butter, milk, and a little minced onion): the mother of all white sauces

Desserts

Baklava (phyllo pastry layered with spices, ground walnuts, almonds, and honey syrup)
Bougatsa (phyllo and apples with butter in a vanilla cream, topped with powdered sugar, and cinnamon)
Galactoboureco (phyllo pastry encircling a vanilla-flavored custard center made with milk, butter, semolina, eggs, and cinnamon syrup)
Kataifi (shredded wheat made with honey, cinnamon, and walnuts)
Melopitta (honey cheesecake)
Payoto (ice cream)
Rizogalo (Macedonian rice pudding)
Tiropetes (cheese tarts)

Avoid **desserts made with butter or an abundance of sugar.**

GREEK DEFENSIVE DINING TIPS

Here are some tips to guide you when eating out in a Greek restaurant:

1. Ask about the ingredients in the dishes you're thinking about ordering.
2. Eat a serving of *horta salata* (Swiss chard, dandelion, or mustard greens) or any other green vegetable daily.
3. Eat *feta, kasseri*, and other fatty or salty cheeses only in small amounts.
4. Avoid *mousaka* and *pastistio*, because these dishes contain *béchamel* (a fatty white cream sauce).
5. Avoid dishes that contain egg yolks.
6. Avoid lamb; it's too fatty to incorporate into a healthful eating plan.

GREEK PHRASES

If you'd like to order a special meal in Greece someday, these phrases will help.

1. ***Please bring some Greek bread.***
   Parakalo, psomi eliniko.

2. ***I'd like a glass of bottled water, please.***
   Parakalo, thelo nero sto boukali.

3. ***I'd like appetizers such as taramousalata*** **and** ***tsasiki.***
   Thelo mezethes san taramousalata kdi tsasiki.

4. ***I would like some stuffed squid, and butterfly shrimp.***
   Thelo kalamaria gemista y garithes.

5. ***Please bring me a serving of the freshest fish available.***
   Parakalo fere mou to pio fresco psari pou ehete.

6. ***Bring me a Greek salad, please.***
   Parakalo, Horiatiki salata.

7. ***I'd like a side dish of mustard greens and fresh vegetables.***
   Thelo mikro piato fresca lahanika ke horta.

8. ***I would like a plate of cold fresh fruit.***
   Thelo ena plato krio fresco fruto.
9. ***I would like some decaffeinated coffee.***
   Thelo cafe horis caffeine.
10. ***The bill, please. Thank you.***
    To logariasmo, parakalo. Evkaristo.

THE BOTTOM LINE

Food is health to the Greeks. It is their survival, and eating good food makes them feel happy. A Greek dining experience takes on a spiritual feeling.

The Greeks truly believe that eating nutritiously will provide them with strength, so it does. That's why Greek restaurants are joyous, and the people in them eat without concern. They dance and sing, and then—without overeating—eat some more. They have a natural relationship with food. You'll never hear Greeks sitting around analyzing what they're eating or why they're eating it—they're too busy enjoying their food.

If you're interested in enjoying healthful meals while traveling, go on to part 3. It will tell you exactly what you need to do.

Kalin orexi! (Enjoy!)

PART 3

▲

Eating Healthfully in Our Friendly Skies

▼

▲

WHILE on vacation, most of us want a break from our usual schedules and customary habits. So, it's common for traveling to lead to overeating and underexercising. On a plane, there's not much to do while sitting in a cramped uncomfortable space for several hours, so, even if you're not hungry and the food looks unappealing, you eat.

The food has already been paid for, I should at least try it, you say to yourself. And, before you know it, you've finished everything including the frosted cake that was set in front of you.

Anyone who flies, but particularly frequent fliers, need to eat right and exercise regularly, no matter where they are, because away-from-home traveling is their way of life. However, figuring out what to eat while in flight can be difficult; it takes planning to stay healthy while traveling.

It's best to think of eating on a plane as you think of eating in a restaurant. You wouldn't accept whatever the waiter decided to bring in a restaurant, would you? Then you shouldn't eat whatever is put in front of you on a plane.

In the following pages you will learn how to order special meals that fit in with your nutritional needs, and how to prevent jet lag so you'll feel good once you get wherever you're going.

Chapter 12

▲

DINING IN THE SKY

FOR many of us traveling is a way of life. Some business people fly on the average of three times a month. Long-distance trips can be ruined when the food is not to your liking or when jet lag sets in and you are unable to function properly. Your business meeting or dream vacation can turn into a nightmare.

It's also not easy to stay slim when traveling regularly. The typical airline lunch or dinner, including dessert, contains 800 calories—more than two-thirds the calories most people need daily—and relatively few nutrients.

Some airlines serve prepackaged frozen processed food that has been popped into the oven, so you're stuck with a meal that isn't particularly tasteful or healthful. Choices such as chicken or beef swimming in gravy are usually available, but —after taking a few bites—you may still be uncertain about which one you are eating.

On most airlines, however, special requests are an option. You can special-order particular foods or drinks you want at no extra charge. Anyone can—whether they fly first class or economy—and they don't have to be a celebrity or the former president of the United States.

People have been known to ask for seedless green grapes in January, noncarbonated mineral water, special formula for their baby, even a birthday cake. Perhaps microwaves will be on board, someday, to heat customers' carryon meals.

Filling customer requests is commonplace to most in-flight catering staffs. Just ask for what you want when you arrange your flight, then confirm twenty-four hours before departure to make sure it has been entered into the computer, and that special item will be there when you want it.

Special Meals

With at least twenty-four hours' notice, airlines are required to offer special meals for all passengers on flights longer than one hour twenty-nine minutes. Most airlines don't publicize this service, however, because in-flight attendants report it causes too much envy from passengers who haven't requested special meals. If people knew their options, however, there would be more happy campers flying our skies.

Ask questions about available meal choices whenever you make flight reservations. On most airlines you can select from kosher, Moslem, and Hindu meals, all designed for those special requirements. Other meal options include diabetic, gluten-free, bland, infant, low-calorie, low-sodium, low-cholesterol, and vegetarian. Any of these may be selected if they suit your nutritional needs or simply because you prefer them. There is no extra charge for these special requests, either.

Airlines hire executive chefs and their assistants, who will prepare food the way you like it. Meals are made in kitchens set up near most airports for that purpose. They are cooked a few hours prior to flight time and held in cooling rooms—because of safety regulations—until they're transported to the airline before takeoff.

Informed frequent flyers who choose a particular airline make standing requests. They're entered into the computer so they'll have the meal(s) they want every time they fly. This service is also free of charge.

Snacks

If you want to avoid retaining water, I recommend skipping the luncheon meat sandwiches and honeyed nuts airlines generally provide as snacks.

Since airlines won't provide special snacks, I suggest you save part of your meal or take along your own healthful snack when traveling. That way you can be sure to have a sandwich, a large fresh pretzel—sold at most airports—some fresh fruit, raw vegetables, low-fat cheese, unbuttered popcorn, or a thermos of hot soup, juice, water, or whatever you want whenever you get hungry or thirsty.

Beverages

If you don't want to carry drinks along, request mineral water, fruit juice, club soda, hot water and lemon, herb tea, or decaffeinated coffee from the flight attendant.

It's important to avoid alcoholic beverages and drinks containing caffeine such as sodas and coffee, particularly while flying, because they are caloric and can dehydrate your skin. I advise my clients to drink one glass of water for every hour inflight to replenish the moisture in their system. They've reported feeling much better.

Exercise Matters—Everywhere

In order to exercise more easily while on board, wear comfortable clothing and walk around the cabin for a few minutes at least once an hour. If it is too difficult to get up because the flight attendants are in the aisles, you can kick off your shoes while seated, roll your feet around a few times in both directions, and contract and relax your leg muscles several times. Innovative airlines are showing exercise videos. During stopovers, or whenever you're permitted to deboard the plane, put your shoes back on and get some exercise walking around the airport.

If you're rambunctious and need more than a walk, some airports have health club facilities with your needs in mind. For a $3 to $10 entrance fee, they provide dressing rooms, showers, and restaurants that serve nutritional meals. Ask the people at the airport information desk about availability. In the future, travelers will carry along gym bags, just in case they run into a flight delay or unexpected layover. These full-service clubs provide indoor tracks, pools, racquetball courts, weights, exercise bikes, treadmills, stair-climbing machines, and—if you're not tired yet—rowing machines.

Since most hotels are also equipped with health club facilities, I recommend you choose one with a workout room, pool, jogging track, or tennis court so you can participate in the sport you enjoy most. Your travel agent can help you locate one.

Some resorts will even deliver exercise equipment to your room for a small fee. For additional exercise, walk to restaurants and your appointments whenever possible.

Menu Command

The Dining in the Sky Menu Command will give you a good idea about which meal to request. Remember these are guidelines, since each airline is different. Some items will be healthful, others won't. I suggest to my clients that they eat what's healthful and leave what's not, as they would in any restaurant. **An asterisk (*) appears next to the meals I recommend.** The others usually contain too much fat, sugar, and salt.

Bland Meal (not fried or highly seasoned foods; designed for people with ulcers). White breads; smooth peanut butter; boiled noodles, mashed potatoes, or rice; pureed carrots, pureed broccoli, avocado, mild salad dressing; melon balls, stewed peach, stewed pear, cranberries; plain yogurt; noncola beverages, milk, juices; butter/margarine and roll.*

Children's Meal (airlines recommend this meal for children under twelve years of age, yet they will provide any meal you prefer). Hamburger, hot dog, canned spaghetti, or peanut-butter-and-jelly sandwich. Granola bar, cookies, cheese, fruit wedge, ice cream, or sherbet is often included. This meal is not recommended because it contains too much fat, sugar, and salt.

Diabetic Meal (does not contain sugar). Boiled beef, chicken, white fish, or turkey; tomato with celery salad or artichoke with pimento, steamed green vegetables; melon wedge, orange slices, apple, strawberries, or pineapple; diet soft drinks or coffee with artificial sweeteners; margarine and roll.*

Fruit Plate (cold plate). Fruit and cheese with bread or crackers. Sometimes a salad and dessert are included. This cold plate is a smart choice for some people since reheating hasn't influenced the flavor of the food.*

Gluten-Free Meal (gluten is the sticky substance that remains in flour when the starch is removed). Prawn cocktail, roast turkey, chicken, or fillet of beef; artichoke with pimento; Boston lettuce with oil-and-vinegar dressing; melon wedge; coffee, tea, low-fat milk, juices, soft drinks; rice cakes, gluten-free bread.*

Hindu Meal (contains no meat). Steamed vegetables, rice, salad; melon, apple wedge, orange slices, strawberries, pineapple; ice cream; coffee, tea, low-fat milk, juices, soft drinks; bread.*

Infant Meal (for infants eight months to two years of age). Strained or finely chopped fruit, meats, and vegetables; milk and juice are available.*

Kosher Meal (contains no pork, and milk and meat dishes are not served together). Beef or chicken, stuffed mushrooms; fruit, vegetable, dessert; coffee, tea, low-fat milk, juices, soft drinks; roll.*

Low-Calorie Meal (sometimes called Travelers' Lighter Choice). Fruit platter, cold seafood platter, meat, fish, poultry, or eggs; green vegetables, unsweetened fruit; coffee, nonfat milk, tea, juices, diet soft drinks; roll and margarine.*

Low-Carbohydrate Meal (high in protein). Meat, fish, or poultry; unsweetened fruits; decaffeinated coffee, diet soft drinks, milk, juice; crackers.*

Low-Cholesterol/Low-Fat Meal. Lean meats, fish, or poultry with the skin removed; noodles, rice, or potatoes; green or yellow vegetables—made with corn, safflower, or soybean oil—melon, apple wedge, orange slices, strawberries, or pine-

***=Recommended**

apple; coffee, tea, nonfat milk, juice, soft drink; whole-grain bread.*

Low-Sodium Meal (contains no added salt). Tomato and cucumber, celery with pimento, Boston and iceberg lettuce, green vegetable, boiled carrots; boiled shrimp, white fish, chicken, or turkey; melon, apple wedge, orange slices, strawberries, or pineapple; coffee, tea, nonfat milk, juices; whole-grain, white bread, unsalted margarine.*

Moslem Meal (contains no pork). Chicken, lamb, or eggplant curry; lettuce, tomato, cucumber with oil-and-vinegar dressing; yellow or green vegetable; fresh or stewed fruit; coffee, tea, nonfat milk, or juice; roll and margarine.*

Postweaning Meal (airlines recommend this for children under two years of age, yet they will provide any meal you prefer). White bread, egg salad, peanut butter and jelly, melon wedge, orange slices, ice cream, milk.*

Seafood Meal. Smoked salmon, smoked oysters, prawns, scallops, or stuffed tomato with tuna; melon or apple wedge, orange slices, strawberries, pineapple; boiled potatoes or noodles; green vegetables, carrots, red cabbage, asparagus, cherry tomato; celery or cucumber with oil-and-vinegar dressing; coffee, tea, nonfat milk, juice, soft drink; roll and margarine. (This meal is not recommended because smoked foods are too salty.)

Vegetarian Meal (recommended for people who want a high-complex-carbohydrate meal and those who avoid meat). Celery with tomato, artichoke with olives, asparagus with pimento, steamed cauliflower, broccoli, grilled tomato; vegetable soup;

*** = Recommended**

sautéed herb vegetables (celery, chopped onion, carrots, red and green pimentos); wild rice; melon or apple wedge, orange slices, strawberries, pineapple; stewed or fresh fruits; coffee, tea, nonfat milk, juice, soda; roll.*

DEFENSIVE DINING IN THE SKY TRAVEL TIPS

1. Eat a nutritious meal before boarding every flight. That way, you won't get on a plane overly hungry, and you will have the willpower to reject food if it's not what you want to eat.
2. Ask questions and order the meal you want when making your plane reservations.
3. Avoid eating excessively salty, fatty, and sugary foods.
4. Drink a glass of water every hour or so to avoid dehydration.
5. Avoid drinking alcoholic beverages and caffeinated beverages; they are extremely dehydrating while flying. Order instead nonfat or low-fat milk, mineral water, club soda, fruit juice, or decaffeinated coffee.
6. Request nonfat or low-fat milk with your coffee rather than the nondairy whiteners that may contain saturated fat.
7. Make an effort not to eat out of boredom or because food has been plopped down in front of you.
8. Avoid the desserts that come with airline meals. They usually contain sugar, coconut oil (a saturated fat) and approximately 400 calories.
9. Get up, move around, and stretch while in flight, or at least exercise in your seat.

The Bottom Line

Carefully select the airline you fly, depending upon what's important to you. Some people expect lousy food and feel satisfied with safe, convenient, on-time flights. Others require good meals in addition to safety while flying.

Airline executives who know that passengers remember good food are the ones whose flights are sold out. Their high standards are maintained by providing their in-flight catering service with an ample budget. They also send their executive chefs on trips to study foreign cuisines and to see what other airline caterers are doing.

Although it's difficult to make airline food delicious, because safety regulations require cool-down and reheating, catering staffs who start out with the best-quality and freshest foods produce tasty and healthful meals.

Thank goodness you no longer need to stay home to stay healthy and slim, but that's only half the battle. Follow the strategies in the next chapter, so you can avoid jet lag and enjoy yourself wherever you are.

Chapter 13

▲

HOW TO AVOID JET LAG

JET lag affects seventy-five percent of the travelers passing through several time zones. Our biological clock, which controls the sleep-wake cycle, remains set at the time back home, and exhaustion sets in. Sometimes it's difficult to get out of bed, let alone enjoy yourself, work, or concentrate.

A client, who runs a consulting practice in Europe and Toronto to teach people how to become successful, told me about his most embarrassing situation related to jet lag. After flying across several time zones he had an early morning business meeting where he was to interview a lady about her goals. While she was answering his question my client fell asleep, snoring with his eyes open for twenty minutes. She tried to awaken him, unsuccessfully, and thought he was extremely ill. Upon awakening, my client said he resumed asking the woman questions, unaware that he had nodded out. Needless to say, he wanted to find out how to avoid jet lag so he wouldn't destroy his business.

A jaunt across the United States can throw our circadian

rhythms off by as much as three hours. A trip to Europe can put us six hours out of sync, and traveling to the Orient can throw us off by as much as twelve hours.

Jet lag tends to hit the hardest when traveling from west to east. For example, it will already be 3:00 P.M. in Italy when you board your 6:00 A.M. Los Angeles flight. When you land in Venice twelve hours later, it will be the middle of the night, but to you it will be early evening.

It shouldn't be surprising, therefore, if the next morning you feel sleepy while touring Piazza San Marco or some other attraction, because for you it will be the middle of the night. When it's bedtime, you could have insomnia. As a rule of thumb, for each one-hour time zone you cross, it can take as much as one day to recuperate.

Anti–Jet Lag Strategies

You don't need to feel out of sorts for a few days or more when you reach your destination because your biological clock has been thrown out of whack. To reduce the effects of jet lag, follow these suggestions:

Traveling East: (shortens your day)

- Prior to your travel date, start shifting the time you eat, sleep, and awaken to the cycle at your destination.
- Go to bed and get up an hour earlier each day for three days prior to departure.
- To obtain the most sleep, make reservations for an early flight.
- Set your watch to the destination time when you board the plane.
- Sit, walk, or run around in the morning sunshine to reset your clock forward.

- Schedule your next day's business meeting, breakfast, or excursion for a late, instead of early, morning time.

Traveling West: (lengthens your day)

- Prior to your travel date, start shifting the time you eat, sleep, and awaken to the cycle at your destination.
- Go to bed and get up an hour later each day for three days before departure.
- Make reservations for a late flight; this allows you to arrive with the least loss of sleep due to the flight.
- Set your watch to the destination time when you board the plane. Psychologically this will help you adjust to your new schedule.
- Get some late-afternoon sunshine when traveling west, because flying westward lengthens your day.
- Schedule your business dinner, meeting, or excursion for an early, rather than a late, time in the evening.

Flying East or West:

- Break up flights through more than three time zones with a one-day layover at an intermediate point.
- Get a good night's sleep the night before you get on a plane.
- Eat lightly while on the plane.
- Take healthful snacks along in case you don't like what's served.
- Avoid alcoholic and caffeinated beverages while on the trip.
- Drink plenty of purified water while on board.
- Exercise and stretch while in flight and at your destination.
- Adopt routines according to local time upon arrival.

- Avoid the American plan offered at some resorts. For a pre-set rate, you can order anything and everything off the menu and that may encourage you to overeat.
- Follow the 12-Step Dining Out Program (see Chapter 3) incorporating your special needs.

The Bottom Line

It takes lots of determination to exercise and eat healthfully while traveling, but now that you have the know-how it's relatively easy. Think of eating on a plane as you think of eating in a restaurant, and dine defensively. Have a great time traveling, eating out in your favorite restaurants, and most importantly be well!

Epilogue

▲

I FELT hunger pangs as I wrote about the many popular cuisines in this book. Many days I'd call a friend and run out for lunch with the appropriate Menu Command in hand, because I wanted to eat the type of food I was writing about. It was exciting because there was so much variety to choose from. Eating moderate amounts of nutritionally sound foods never seemed boring and my weight didn't fluctuate.

You, too, can eat out as often as you'd like, without going off your eating plan. Just be sure to take *Not "Just a Salad"* along as your guide. Menu Command will liberate you from the greasy, salty, sugary foods often served in restaurants. With so many delicious options to choose from, I'm confident you'll start eating more healthfully.

And, if you slip up or decide to splurge once in a while, simply go back on your healthful eating plan with the next item you eat! Fortunately, when it comes to nutrition, it's truly what you do most of the time that matters.

It's a question of balance. If one meal contains more fat than you'd like, eat more leanly the next. The trick is not to make overeating on a particular occasion an excuse to blow your diet. Many people think they'd follow a more healthful eating plan if they just had enough willpower. But, *wantpower* is what they need. Their desire to stay healthy needs to be greater than their desire to eat foods off their plan.

Each time you eat, remember that no one is either on or off a diet all the time. And, no one eats unconsciously. The decision to follow a healthful or unhealthful life-style is a choice each of us makes on a minute-to-minute, forkful-by-forkful basis.

Now, or at your next opportunity, go out to one of your favorite restaurants and order something good that's good for you too. You deserve the best!

Index

▲